What do we do in the sudden mom
turn? Leanne's journey, from the sho
cer to the treatment and recovery, bec
and renewal of hope in the presence and power of God through the
toughest times. It will move you and encourage you to put your
hand in the hand of the God who holds you, loves you and will
never let you go.

*Revd Chris Cartwright, Elim general superintendent*

In her book, Leanne takes us on a very personal journey and shows us
how the mountain of breast cancer was removed with mustard-seed
faith. Her story is relatable, thoughtful and unflinchingly honest.
As you read, you'll be inspired and challenged to face your own
mountains with grace and strength.

*Revd Dr Tania Harris, director of God Conversations*

Leanne writes with inspiring honesty about how God's mighty
hands brought about change, direction and healing in her life. Her
brave, tenacious and courageous decision to constantly trust God –
encouraging us to do the same – is as compelling as it is inspiring.

As you thoughtfully follow Leanne's story, take a moment to
keep reminding yourself, whatever life throws at us – we're safe in
his hands.

*Amy Summerfield, CEO of Kyria Network,*
*head of development at Skylark International, leader at*
*Zeo Church, Hitchin, itinerant speaker and leadership coach*

This is a remarkable book about a remarkable family that will impact and help many. It moved me to tears at times but also inspired
me with hope and wonderful insights into how to hold the hand of
Jesus through every storm. Leanne's powerful writing opens such a
personal story with honesty and courage that will inspire you too.

*Eric Gaudion, retired Elim pastor and author*

I had the privilege of serving alongside Leanne on Elim's national women's team, Aspire, for over a decade.

Leanne is an exemplary leader and her new book, *With These Hands*, will take you on a journey of faith in the face of fear and uncertainty.

Honest, frank and deeply moving it will both challenge and inspire.

Leanne has told her story with great courage and grace, epitomizing the woman I have come to know.

*Julia Derbyshire, co-leader at City Gates Church, Ilford*

If you are facing obstacles that seem overwhelming, this book will be the perfect read. Leanne's vulnerability brings a safety and comfort as she shares her journey in trusting God in the midst of the unknown. Sometimes we just need to be reminded that no matter what we face, we are never left alone and hope can be found even in the most daunting of circumstances. I highly recommend this book to anyone who needs to be reminded that God is trustworthy even when we don't understand the difficulties life can often bring. This book is not only for those who have walked through illness but I also encourage those who are currently facing loss of any kind to read through Leanne's story, as I have no doubt you will be encouraged!

*Christy Wimber, author, former senior pastor, international speaker,*
*overseer of global church planting for Friends churches*

This is a wonderful, uplifting testimony of how Leanne has personally experienced God's gentle but powerful hands, especially in the tough times. Regardless of your own journey, this book will encourage you and inspire greater faith to believe that God can miraculously intervene in your situation too. Woven throughout Leanne's story are practical keys to successfully traverse trials, and fresh perspectives on what matters most in life.

*Greta Peters, co-founder of SpiritLife Ministries, New Zealand*

# With These Hands

## Holding on to God in the Storms of Life

Leanne Mallett

**Authentic**

# Contents

# Foreword

I clearly remember a moment a few years ago when I came across a particular proverb from the Bible. I have no idea if I'd actually read it before, but suddenly in this memorable moment it hit me between the eyes in a powerful and persistent way. What was this potent proverb? It says:

'Hope deferred makes the heart sick, but a longing fulfilled is a tree of life.' (Prov. 13:12)

Well, those wise words resonated deeply with me. They chimed with so many occasions or seasons of my life where I had experienced loss or disappointment or delay. And perhaps the words resonate with you too. All of us experience times when our hope seems to be deferred. Sometimes what we hope for is delayed for a short time. But sometimes we experience a more chronic hope deferral, when things just don't work out as planned. And yes, it's perfectly possible for our hearts to get a little sick and for our soul to become tired in the process. It's understandable. Life can be hard work sometimes.

Of course, testing seasons are not unusual seasons. And as Christians we are not immune to them, in fact, quite the opposite – the Bible tells us to expect and to prepare for suffering after all. But these difficult times also challenge us to consider what it is our hope is *really in* and what it is that *we really long for*. If we are painfully and grittily honest with ourselves, many of us rather hope that God will solve all our problems in exactly the way we'd like and in precisely the timescale of our choosing! Our basic longing is often that life just gets sorted out. Or is that just me?

But here's the thing: life is not a fairy tale with a guaranteed happy ending and God is not a divine slot machine, where we put a prayer in and get a solution out. Rather, God is the God of relationship. *That* is where our hope lies. And this means that our hope does not need to ultimately be deferred and our longing *can* be fulfilled whatever our circumstances – because God promises to walk with us and never leaves us. That certain hope is the only real cure for our heartsickness.

And don't you just love that the Bible is jam-packed with stories of people who have faced challenges, tough times and disappointments? Thank God that the Bible never steers away from the realities of life. As we read Scripture, we see that sometimes circumstances work out well for people but sometimes they just don't. But each time, we can see what God does in people and through people and how he reveals his goodness and love along the way.

This is why I never tire of reading stories – in the Bible, but also stories of other people. We learn so much as we share stories of life and faith, especially as people navigate life's unexpected ups and downs. And this is also why I *love* this book written by Leanne. It is an honest and insightful testimony written about a particularly tough season of life. Many of us will have experienced a similar moment where we (or somebody we love) received a diagnosis and life turned upside-down in that instant. Leanne doesn't dumb down the challenges she has faced and doesn't gloss over the tough questions she has asked along the way. Neither does she pretend that her journey has been glorious or easy in every moment. I am so grateful for that.

But that said, Leanne's story is a story of hope.

The pages you are about to read have been an incredible encouragement to me, and I am sure they will be to you. And even if the specifics of Leanne's challenges and experiences are different from yours, I feel confident you will resonate as you consider the various battles you are facing or have faced. I pray you will gain strength and glean wisdom from somebody who has had to walk an incredibly uncertain path (with no guaranteed happy ending), and who has chosen to do so in dependence on God. I would testify along with Leanne that God really is always good, even when life is quite bad. And I also thank God for where she is now, and how God is using her in this new season.

In summary, I am so grateful that Leanne chose to put pen to paper (or fingers to keyboard). As an author, I know it is an incredibly vulnerable thing to do. You wonder – what will people think? What if folks disagree or have different outcomes or different experiences? It is brave to be so honest in such a public way. But if you know anything about Leanne, you will know she is a treasure of a human being and a beautifully brave woman, who humbly encourages everyone she meets. I appreciate Leanne so much. She is not telling her story to draw attention to herself or how courageous she is; she is telling it to draw attention to the God who attended to her heartsickness and fulfilled her longing to know him in every circumstance.

What a wonderful testimony. What a great encouragement. What a good God.

And what a great book!

Cathy Madavan

# Introduction

The year 2021 was a year that many of us will remember for the ongoing Covid-19 pandemic and many lockdowns. It was a time that brought disappointment, frustration, heartache and change for so many people. As a nation, we had to adjust to a new way of living that none of us were really prepared for. We had to rethink old methods and quickly adapt and embrace new ones. However, for me, it also became the most challenging year of my life as I faced even more uncertainty for the future.

Just before Christmas 2020, I was diagnosed with breast cancer and, the following year, I embarked on a journey that taught me so much about myself, life and the God that I serve.

I have been a Christian since the age of eight years old and have experienced the love of God throughout the different seasons of my life. However, navigating this unexpected health battle, I realized there was so much I had yet to experience about him. As I sat here, reflecting on a successful but challenging year of treatment, I found myself at a place where I didn't want to 'sit' on what God had showed me. During this time of recovery I have wondered whether my story and the things I've learned will help and encourage others going through similar battles.

After sharing my story with a few people, I was prompted a few times to write a book. I prayed and left it with the Lord but the prompting to do it never really went away. Then one night I just couldn't sleep and I knew this was something that maybe God was asking me to do so I wanted to be obedient. Writing a book is something I have always wanted to do but I never thought I would be writing one about such a life-changing experience.

This book tells a story not only of my journey with breast cancer, but also of what God can do through and in you if you just trust him and allow him to work in your life. While going through this season, the hands of God really stood out to me. I learned about the many ways in which he uses his mighty hands to bring about change, direction and healing. I can see the ways in which he used them to comfort me, move me, lead me, hold me, steady me, uphold me and mould me. As I started to reflect on this season, I recognized his fingerprints have actually been on many situations throughout my life that have led me to this point. I want to share some of these in this book as I can see how God taught me things in my early years that were so key for me in this season of my life.

Sharing my story is not aimed at bringing sympathy or attention to myself, or because I think my story is more important or more difficult than anyone else's. I understand that there are many women who have gone through breast cancer and similar treatments to mine and as you read this book you will relate to some of my experiences. There are many people reading this book who have battled and endured tough health crises and some who are going through those things right now. I want you to know that each and every one of you are true inspirations and my prayer is that you will find comfort and strength with some of the things I have shared.

Our stories are powerful and we should not hold back in sharing what Jesus has done in our lives and the things he has taught us.

I know not everyone's journey is the same and each one of us can deal with such things differently too, there is no right or wrong way. My account of what I went through I know won't reflect everyone's feelings or responses to similar experiences. Not everyone's journey ends the same and we can often struggle with the different outcomes in life. We all know of loved ones who have endured terrible hardships and the outcome was not what we expected – life can often seem so unfair. Sometimes we have no answers other than we have to trust God's timing for our lives and know he is in total control, whether we have earthly understanding or not.

My prayer is that sharing what God taught me and what I learned in my life up until this point will not only help and encourage you in your journey, but also help others travelling with you in it. I have written this book so that you will know how much you mean to God and how he is just there waiting with arms wide open. If my story encourages one person or points someone to Jesus then this book has completed all that it set out to do.

Towards the end of each chapter, I will write about 'His Hands' and what I learned about them in relation to that part of my story. I am sure as you read these sections you will not only read my experiences and reflections but you will also recognize times in your own life when God's hands have helped you – even when you may not have realized it.

At the end of each chapter I will also encourage you to 'Take a Moment' – to stop and reflect on your life right now and be open to what God may be saying to you in this season. Many reading this book may not have a relationship with Jesus but, as you read my story, I pray that you will learn something about a loving heavenly Father who is just waiting for you to take hold of his hand.

# 1

# Mountains

It was October 2020 and my husband, Darren, my daughter, Abi and I were travelling to Cardiff in Wales as Abi had an appointment to try on wedding dresses. She was getting married the following September and finding a wedding dress during the Covid-19 lockdown was proving quite difficult. No sooner were restrictions lifted and shops open than it would all change again in a matter of weeks, so when we had a window to go dress-hunting, we took it! Going wedding-dress shopping with Abi was something I had dreamed about for years so there was a real excitement in the car that day for both of us.

Both Darren and I are from Cardiff and so we had done this journey from Hereford many times to visit family. Jack, my son, was also studying at university there so we were quite used to the country roads along the way. As we were driving along the familiar roads, Abi and I suddenly became aware of the huge mountains that were all around us – we gasped at the magnitude of them! Darren was driving and I don't think he quite understood why today these mountains were so special so he carried on singing to worship songs in the car while we shared in our 'mountain excitement'. It was almost as if Abi and I were seeing these mountains for the first time and I wondered why we hadn't taken much notice of them before. That day for some reason the mountains stood out. It was almost like one of those moments when you look up and start noticing the beauty around you – beauty that had been there all along.

I started to wonder whether God was speaking to me about a sermon or message about mountains that he wanted me to share in church. God can speak to us in many ways – whether that is through reading the Bible, through others, or hearing his voice ourselves. A friend of mine, Tania Harris, has written a book called *God Conversations*.[1] It's a book of stories of how God speaks to us and what his voice sounds like. I am quite a visual learner and so I often find that God speaks to me through things that I see or come across during my day – I love it when it happens! There have been many times when something has stood out to me more than usual on a journey – whether a slogan on a lorry, a traffic sign or just a scenario on the road, but I would get drawn to it a bit more than usual – almost like a nudge from God to take note. I would often find these 'nudges' became the start of a sermon for church or a message that I needed to bring somewhere and God would elaborate further on them. Sometimes, I would 'bank' what I saw as I sensed it would be relevant for something or someone in the future.

Having faith that God could 'move a mountain' was something that immediately came to me and as we looked at the mountains from the car, we recalled that Scripture in the Gospel of Matthew where it talks about having faith to move mountains.

There was a mountain in the distance that we were particularly drawn to that day. Due to the angle of the car, it almost reduced downwards among the trees as we drove towards it. I was so excited as I captured the whole thing on my mobile phone and I imagined how this video would be a great illustration to the sermon that was unravelling.

The mountain seemed to disappear before our eyes (although I know it actually didn't!) and that moment would be significant for me personally in the months that lay ahead – and I had no idea.

**His Hands**

When we think about those impossible situations in our lives right now or maybe in the lives of others, it is easy to put limits on the outcome. We usually default to the natural way of looking at things. It's easy to put faith in God for the things we know can change but I really believe that, when we read the following verse from the Gospel of Matthew, Jesus wants us to have faith for the impossible. 'He replied, "Because you have so little faith. Truly I tell you, if you have faith as small as a mustard seed, you can say to this mountain, 'Move from here to there,' and it will move. Nothing will be impossible for you"' (Matt. 17:20, NIV).

If we have to think of an example of anything in this world that is unmovable, it's mountains! If I stood at the foot of a mountain today and commanded it to move, I am not sure there would be an ounce in me that would expect it to. However, this example was used to illustrate the point that even though we can be faced with situations that we know are 100 per cent impossible, we just need a tiny amount of faith that God can change the outcome. We need to have faith in who God is and what he is able to do. The verse says: 'Nothing will be impossible for you.'

Due to travelling around for our ministry work, we have lived in a number of houses. When we moved from Bridgend in Wales to Salisbury in England the house price jump was so big it meant we couldn't afford to buy a house there, so we rented. The first house we rented was a brand new build and, as it was the last house on the street to be constructed, surrounding it was still a lot of rubble, stones and cement. One day I was getting out of my car on the driveway and I noticed among the rubble at the back of the house, in a dusty, barren, rocky area, a beautiful poppy had sprung up. Among the grey, dull background where there was no greenery or hint of any growth, a beautiful bright red flower had bloomed. It stood out! As it was in such an unexpected place, it caught my eye.

Two years later, we moved again to a rented property in the country. This property used to be a huge pub on a country road but they had recently converted it to about five bespoke houses so when we moved in they were still completing the building work on one of them. The garden again had lots of rubble around it and the ground was very stony. Then, some weeks later as I walked outside the house, there among the rubble a daffodil had just popped up in the most random of places. As I looked around, I noticed another group of daffodils had also sprung up among the stones. It was unusual as it was also the wrong time of year for daffodils to bloom, so again, it caught my eye.

At that particular time I was missing home and I really felt God speak to me about blooming where I was planted, but these flowers had an even greater message. Both the poppy and the daffodil popped up and bloomed in areas that you would not expect any flowers to grow and perhaps in seasons that were not expected. The stone, rubble areas were not the ideal environment for any growth. I would even describe it as 'impossible'. Yet, as those flowers stood bright and bold, I was reminded that God can do anything. He can bring forth life where it seems barren. He can do the unexpected in any situation, in any season, because he is God.

This got me thinking about those men and women in the Bible that God chose to do exploits for him – those who perhaps felt under-qualified, unpopular or inadequate. Those who may have been looked down on because of their jobs, their age or their past.

Moses perhaps wasn't the perfect man for the job but God spoke to him in an unexpected way and told him he was going to lead the Israelites out of Egypt into the promised land – what a moment that must have been! God knew what was in Moses and knew he could do the task ahead.

Rahab, a Canaanite woman and a prostitute, was perhaps not the person most expected to secure the safety of the Israelites as they enter the promised land but, despite her past and her choice of profession, she was chosen to do this. God loves us whoever we are and can use us regardless of our past.

In Luke 19, we read that out of all the people in the crowd, Jesus chose to go to Zacchaeus' house for tea. I'm sure the people in that village that day would have been shocked by his choice of a dishonest tax collector; however, Jesus demonstrated that he sees those who think they are not worthy or not seen. He publicly showed that who you are and what you do doesn't make you any less loved or chosen.

God doesn't eliminate us from doing his exploits based on our age or experience. David was a young boy who wasn't considered important and yet God chose him to bring down a giant. Jeremiah was a young boy who felt inadequate, but God used him to speak his words to the people. Even Mary who was the mother of Jesus was chosen at a young age, and not even married, to give birth to the Son of God.

The Bible is full of stories of God using unexpected people to do extraordinary things and it is an example of how our God can work in and through us today. Throughout the Bible, he shows us how he can do the impossible and use the unexpected. Therefore when we look at difficult situations or look at our own inabilities we must remember that God can do far more than we can naturally imagine. Sometimes we need that reminder of how big our God is.

I recently learned that there are approximately four hundred thousand different types of flowering plant species in the world. I was also amazed to learn that there are not only nine planets in our solar system but an estimation of at least one hundred billion planets in our Milky Way alone. Just take in the magnitude of this for a couple of moments – think about the detail of every flower and then the size of the billions of planets. If God made all these and hung all the billions of planets in space, your problem is not too difficult for him and is certainly not impossible.

The book of Psalms reminds us that the skies are a reflection of his craftsmanship: 'The heavens declare the glory of God; the skies proclaim the work of his hands' (Ps. 19:1, NIV). Just look around and look up and see how mighty his hands are. We should never limit God by thinking of what human hands are capable of doing. We have a supernatural God and the works of his hands are incredible. His hands can therefore move mountains!

**Take a Moment . . .**

Why not write down all those things that are troubling you right now?

Have you resigned yourself to the idea that some of these issues are impossible and you have almost given up on believing for a breakthrough?

Before you continue to read on, ask God to show you areas of your life where you may be limiting him because you can't naturally see a way through.

As you reflect on these things, also reflect on the beauty and detail of creation – the same hands that hung the stars in space can move your mountain.

# 2

# Be Strong

A few weeks after our drive to Cardiff, it was a cold but sunny November morning and I was driving to the doctor's. For a few weeks I had been experiencing pain in my right breast. The pain wasn't going away and I wondered whether I had pulled a muscle in my chest. I had tried a few weeks of pain-killers but the pain was persistent and seemed to be getting worse. I decided to make an appointment with my GP as I knew I needed this to be checked out.

Growing up, I always feared the worst with any pain. If I had a pain in my body, I would literally go to the worst-case scenario and convince myself I had it. I would go on the internet and type in the symptoms and, even if I didn't have all the symptoms related to what popped up then, you could guarantee the following day I would. This fear used to grip me every time and I would be so convinced I had all those terrible things.

Over the years I realized it was becoming a tactic of the enemy to instil fear in me and to rob me of my peace. Fear can so easily paralyse us, and I recognized I was starting to live my life with all these fears dominating how I was thinking and living. Therefore, I tried to put things in place to prevent fear controlling my life.

I first stopped searching symptoms on the internet and, second, rather than worry about any aches and pains and allowing fear to grip me, I would face any illnesses head on and get things checked out. So often, the fears and worries I had would amount to nothing but I would be carrying them around with me like unwanted baggage. I was too afraid to know the truth of the situation in case it was something I didn't want to hear.

Knowing the truth really does set you free in so many ways. How often do we give fear a 'seat at our table' or a 'place in our home'? Allowing this to take root in our thoughts and actions is like entertaining an unwelcome guest.

'Be alert and of sober mind. Your enemy the devil prowls around like a roaring lion looking for someone to devour' (1 Pet. 5:8, NIV). This verse tells us that we should be alert! Fear is probably one of the biggest tools in the devil's toolbox to try and stop us moving forward. Here in this verse it warns us how the enemy operates. As when sniffer dogs are let in to sniff out dangerous substances or objects, we need to 'sniff out' those thoughts and mindsets that are not from God.

Over the years, although I have put safety measures in place to 'sniff out' when this is happening to me, it doesn't stop the fear from trying to find a way in. Therefore, putting on the armour of God daily is key in dealing with all that gets thrown at us. In the book of Ephesians it tells us what we can do to protect ourselves: 'Put on the full armour of God, so that you can take your stand against the devil's schemes' (Eph 6:11, NIV).

As I drove to the doctor's that morning, I had the words 'be strong' come to me. It was so clear. Again, I wondered if this was God giving me the title of my next few sermons or if this was a reminder that I needed to face a fear head on and be strong that day.

As I lay on the couch in the doctor's room, there was a silence as she examined me. I had convinced myself there wouldn't be anything there so I was waiting to hear those words. When the doctor finished, I sat on the edge of the couch as she explained that she had felt a thickening.

I needed reassurance in that moment so I mentioned that I had pain, and that had to be a good sign, surely? I had read somewhere that often pain in the breast is a good indicator that it is not sinister. The doctor agreed it could be a reassuring sign, but she also stated that I 'needed to go there too', meaning I needed to prepare myself for the fact that this could possibly be breast cancer.

It all seemed a bit surreal, as though this shouldn't be happening to me and it was some sort of mistake. I quickly realized there was nothing I could do to change her mind or convince her it was something else. There wasn't much reassurance coming back, even though I had tried to get it.

Although my investigations were classed as urgent, due to Covid-19 I was told it could take up to two weeks just to get an initial appointment at the breast clinic. As I left the surgery all I kept thinking was that there was no way I could wait that long. I knew that even after the initial appointment I would probably need further tests and the waiting would be agony for me.

I drove home from the doctor's in a bit of a daze and as I walked through the front door, Darren was waiting for me on the sofa. It was just us, and he locked my eyes looking for a reassuring look back. As I sat down and explained what the doctor had said to me, I could feel the panic starting to rise. All those years I had my strategies to face fear but this was now one of my biggest fears becoming a reality. I knew waiting two weeks would be difficult for me so I spent most of that morning searching for private health care appointments with a hope I could be seen quicker.

An appointment was made at the Nuffield Hospital in Cheltenham for three days later. There, I could be seen by a breast surgeon and have a scan. I knew I had to do it this way as Christmas was just over two weeks away and I could imagine that staff would be limited in this season, especially with the demands of Covid-19 on the NHS. I knew this could be hanging over me into the New Year and I needed to know I was OK so that we could all have a lovely Christmas as a family.

The breast surgeon rang me before my appointment. He was so lovely and he reassured me that it was such a good sign that I was having pain but he needed to scan me to make sure. I felt much calmer following our chat and was grateful that he sounded so nice and could fit me in so quickly. God knew the type of doctor I needed and I could sense he was going ahead of me already.

## His Hands

Those words 'be strong' that came to me on the way to the doctor stayed with me throughout this season of my life. They continually came back to me, when I needed strength to face something. When someone tells you to 'be strong' in a difficult situation, it is so easy to say but not so easy in practice.

Bodybuilders don't gain strength in a moment. There have been weeks and months of training, they build strength over time. Weightlifters' muscles need to be strong and ready for when they lift the weight. If I was to step up and even attempt to lift weights right now, it would be a bit embarrassing as I haven't trained and I would fail miserably. That day I felt I was being told in advance to 'be strong', to get myself ready.

I have always loved the story in the Bible of the man who built his house on the rock and the man who built his house on sand. I remember the pictures in my childhood Bible storybooks of a happy man standing by his house on a rock, and a sad man looking at his house in bits, standing on sand. I don't think I fully understood what the story meant apart from feeling sorry for the sad man. However, it wasn't actually the structure of the house that was the problem but rather what it was standing on. The man who built his house on the rock soon learned that the foundations were the key factor in the strength of his house. Sadly, the sand man realized he had made a big mistake.

I had made a decision years ago to build 'Leanne', my house, on the rock, on Jesus, and in these moments of uncertainty, those very foundations that I had built my life on were being tested. Choosing to make God the Lord of your life doesn't exempt you from life's storms or the elements. Through this season I still experienced fear and trembling, I still experienced panic. I felt the 'elements', the effects the storm brought, but I could have that inner peace because I knew he was with me in the storm.

Those houses that stood on the rock and sand both faced the elements at the same time. The house on the rock didn't have a special canopy over it protecting it, it faced the weather like the other house. It was the importance of what it was standing on that was the point of the illustration.

As Christians, we face the same storms and troubles in life as everyone else – we aren't excluded or exempt because we choose to live our lives for Jesus. However, when the storms come, we know whom we are standing on and with. Scripture tells us that we will have troubles here on earth but we can have peace knowing whose hands we are in: 'I have told you these things, so that in me you may have peace. In this world you will have trouble. But take heart! I have overcome the world' (John 16:33, NIV).

Although I would often fear that any pain I felt was something serious like cancer, I could never imagine what it would be like to actually face this head on. Due to the fact that I used to be so gripped with the fear of such things while I was growing up, I assumed I would just crumble and fall apart. However, even though I felt those 'elements', I started to fill my mind with the promises given to me in God's word. Those words became more real to me than ever and I could lean on them. Verses reminding me who God is and what he can do soon became a reality to me. For years, I had read these verses, preached about them, encouraged others with them and believed that they could bring healing, but suddenly the power of these words became so real to me.

A Scripture that I held on to right from the start was from the book of Isaiah and it reminded me where I was situated:

> So do not fear, for I am with you;
> do not be dismayed, for I am your God.
> I will strengthen you and help you;
> I will uphold you with my righteous right hand.

> (Isa. 41:10, NIV)

I can testify that God took hold of my hand at the beginning and upheld me with his righteous right hand. He grabbed hold of me in those moments and steadied me on that rock as he told me to be strong. I felt a security like I'd never known before. There was still uncertainty about the outcome at this stage, but what I did know was that he was holding me tight.

In Joshua 1:9 we read another reminder to 'Be strong and courageous', but what I love about that Scripture is, it doesn't just tell us that and leave it there, it tells us why we can be strong and courageous: 'For the L ORD your God will be with you wherever you go.'

What a comfort that is! When others commented on how strong I was throughout this journey, I knew my strength wasn't my own at all. It was as though, as I was about to lift weights in a gym, someone had come behind me and lifted them for me, and I know that was God.

When troubles come our way what a comfort that we can find refuge in him and he gives us the strength that we need.

> The L ORD is my rock, my fortress and my deliverer;
>     my God is my rock, in whom I take refuge,
>         my shield and the horn of my salvation, my stronghold.
>                                                 (Ps. 18:2, NIV)

A rock, fortress, shield and stronghold are places where you are safe from attack. The Lord is described as all of these things in this verse and this reassures us that when troubles come our way we can take refuge, in him.

**Take a Moment . . .**

If you haven't built your life upon Jesus, maybe ask yourself now whether you would like him to be Lord of your life.

There is no greater security than building your life on the one who made you. If you have never even prayed before maybe ask God to reveal himself to you and show you what you mean to him as you continue to read my story.

# 3

# Behind the Wall

I was brought up in a loving, Christian home and every Sunday we would go back and forth to church a few times that day attending all the different services. This was our normal routine and it was the day in the week I loved. My parents were involved in church life in Cardiff and both my brother and I had a good group of friends there while we were growing up.

I was a typical girly girl and loved dolls and playing schools with my teddies. I always wanted to be a school teacher and my teddies would often be lined up on my bed, and I would take the class register. I would be in my bedroom all day playing teachers, reading them stories and using a chalkboard. Even though my brother, Leighton, had no clue, I would make him the headmaster and he would often come out of his bedroom to find one of my dolls outside his door where I had sent them to him for being naughty.

Although at home I was chatty and probably even described as 'bossy' by Leighton, in school I was the opposite. I loved school but I was a quiet and somewhat shy pupil. My school reports every year would usually say, 'Leanne must participate more in class.'

The school system in those days meant your results and grades were based solely on your exam results, and so even though I loved school and did well, I didn't really excel in exams. I found if I revised too early on I would forget it all, so I cram-revised a few days before, which just didn't work. I always tried really hard and did my best but I'd end up so frustrated as I felt my grades didn't reflect my ability. I loved to write essays but I had no confidence in speaking out in class. I was that child at the back who hardly said a word, I worried about saying the wrong thing. I would fear saying something stupid and being the laughing-stock of whole class. If a teacher picked on me to answer a question, everything in me wanted to hide. I didn't have much confidence in my answers so would sit there in silence, often with a friend whispering the answer to me until I was brave enough to speak.

I remember that in my French lessons there were two seats hidden behind a wall that jutted out, and I would run to these every time. It was great as the French teacher would forget I was there. I would sit there, listening to what was being taught, but she never saw me. I was so happy in those lessons. Until one day she gave back my French homework and written on it said something like:

1.  Leanne, Good work.
2.  Cover your book.
3.  Do not sit behind the wall.

Busted! From that moment, I had to come out of hiding and I guess over the years that's what God has done in my life. He's taken my hand and led me out from behind the wall in many ways.

I left school with a couple of O-levels and a bunch of CSE qualifications. I chose not to further my studies because I just wanted to get a job and start earning. I remember my first job was as a filing clerk for a well-known insurance company. In those days paper files were kept, and when a member of staff needed a file, they would shout out, 'Can I have a file, please?' and it was our job as filing clerks to go and find that file in the filing room. It used to frustrate me no end as the files were hardly ever in the right places so you knew as you were searching for them in a long, dusty, cramped filing room that it was a waste of time. I would usually have to go back and explain that the file was not there. Each time I walked up to the member of staff, I would find myself blushing – I was so shy. Inside there was a Leanne who was chatty and even mischievous, desperate to be confident in my ability, but instead I came across so quiet and unconfident. I was 'shy', and this was a label I had firmly fixed on myself. I believed that was who I was and I would always be this way.

Over the next thirteen years, I worked in an administration role for the NHS and, over time, my confidence slowly grew. My blushing stopped and I was known for playing many practical jokes on people in the office. I probably spent more time chatting and being mischievous in those days than I did doing my work. However, I still didn't like the spotlight to be on me. They used to do presentations for birthdays and special milestones so when it was my turn I would beg them not to make me do a speech and somehow, each time, I managed to avoid it.

In June 1996, I married my childhood sweetheart, Darren. Our parents attended an Elim church, then known as the City Temple, but now City Church, Cardiff. They would hang out together while growing up, so when they got married and had children we often went on day trips as families and spent a lot of time together. As we had been born only nine days apart, Darren and I were dedicated at church as babies on the same day and I often smile, thinking how God must have looked down on us that day and said, 'Little do they know what I have planned for them together!'

Darren and I were a part of the big youth group at the church and we were the best of friends growing up. During our teens we became boyfriend and girlfriend, but in those days you would go out together and literally three weeks later you would finish and go out with someone else. We went out with other people for a while and I think it was all very innocent, but one time we were meant to be 'boyfriend and girlfriend' and to my horror he kissed another girl behind my back. That was it for me! (We do laugh about it now but for a time it was great as a throwback to win any arguments.) It took poor Darren six years before I agreed to be his girlfriend again. He tried everything but I wouldn't budge. I think everyone could see we would end up together, and eventually we fell back into one another's arms.

Following our wedding, Darren started his training for ministry. Even as a child he always wanted to be a pastor, and so over the next few years he trained with the Elim Pentecostal denomination.

During his training, in February 1999, we had our first child, Abigail. Abi was born almost ten weeks prematurely due to me having pre-eclampsia, a life-threatening pregnancy condition. At just over thirty weeks, I was filling up with water and my blood pressure was extremely high. The doctors decided Abi needed delivering as my organs were starting to really suffer and things were not looking good for her or me. She was born weighing 3lbs 3ozs (1.45kg).

During those ten weeks of living in the University Hospital of Wales, while Abi was in the neonatal unit, our faith grew to another level. We were not sure if she was going to survive, and it was during this time we experienced God working a miracle before our eyes as he pulled her through those initial battles. It was such a rollercoaster, and seeing her struggle for her life in the intensive care unit is a sight we will never forget. God had his hand on her right from the start and to see her now flourishing as a young adult makes us so thankful.

In January 2001, I gave birth to Jack, who was another precious gift to us. Jack completed our family. I thank God for the two wonderful children that he has blessed us with, and they constantly make us proud.

Moving around in ministry is not always easy on children as it can mean settling and then being unsettled again a few years later. I am so proud of how they coped with the changes and grateful that God has had his hand on them both while they were growing up. There have been many times that I have been so worried about them settling into new schools and making new friends, and then I would see God's hand put things in place just at the right time for them.

While Darren was training for ministry, we led the eighteen-to-thirties young people's group at the City Temple in Cardiff, where we had attended with our families growing up. I quickly realized that being married to a pastor (or training pastor) often meant there was an expectation that his wife would be involved publicly too. We would go to other churches as part of his training and I was often asked to do a Bible reading or prayer. As described previously, public speaking was completely out of my comfort zone, and even doing simple Bible readings was something I felt I just couldn't do. Even though I had grown in confidence as I started work, I was still naturally shy. I wanted to be able to do these things but I would say 'no' at every opportunity presented to me. My reply would automatically be 'It's not me, sorry' or 'I'm too shy'. It was almost as if this was my default response and I didn't even entertain another option.

I remember on one occasion Darren was leading at the front of the youth group and he randomly asked me to pray. I don't know whether he thought putting me on the spot was the best way to kick me out of my comfort zone, or that it would make me face my fears, but let's just say he didn't do that again! I remember freezing on the spot, giving him a knowing look, and shaking my head in refusal.

I managed to avoid these situations for some time. Then one day, when I was pregnant with Jack, I thought to myself, I need to get over this! I wanted to do these things so I needed to say 'yes' to opportunities given to me. I finally agreed to speak and share some things I had learned in my faith journey at the eighteen-to-thirties meeting. Moving up to the front that evening was equivalent to leaping out of a plane eighty thousand feet high for me. I stepped up to the lectern in fear and trembling, relying totally on God to help me, and to my surprise I managed to get through it without fainting! God held my hand with his and I knew he was the one who enabled me to do it.

I guess over the next few years I learned that, even though I was naturally shy, experiencing what God could do through me if I simply trusted him excited me. Even though I was still terrified after every 'yes', I committed to my confidence-growing as it was now based in him, not me. I realized the more I said 'yes', the more opportunities came my way. Job opportunities working for Christian charities and organizations opened up for me. I had a heart to serve and help people, and I also loved administration and organization. Therefore, being in roles where I could use my administration skills for organizations to show the love of Jesus was really fulfilling for me.

In 2003, we moved to Bridgend in Wales to replant an Elim church. We had heard clearly from God about this move and we were so excited. I think, for some, it was hard to understand why we would want to leave the comforts of a large, resourceful church in the centre of a capital city to go to a small town with a church that was struggling. The church was about to close, but we felt God stirring us about going to rebuild it with him. We stayed connected to the church in Cardiff for encouragement and support, and a small team came with us to Bridgend to help us do the work there.

The church in Bridgend desperately needed a new building and the congregation had reduced to a few faithful members. We were so excited to see what God was going to do and we love a challenge, so we moved to the area and grew to love the place and the people quickly. Although it was tough, we learned lessons in this place of training in ministry that grounded us and have stayed with us ever since. I often re-call it as our 'boot camp experience'. It was here that I began preaching and ministering alongside Darren, and we all, as a team, saw God move in powerful ways during the eight years we were there.

Not long after we moved to Bridgend I left my job working for the NHS in Cardiff and became an administrator for a large nursery near where we lived. One day, however, I unex-pectedly had a phone call from a Christian youth charity ask-ing whether I would be interested in working for them as their finance manager. The funny thing about this story is that in school, mathematics was probably one of my worst subjects. My brain did not seem wired for numbers and so finance was not an area that excited me, or I excelled in! To this day, I have no idea why they thought of me when seeking to fill that role but for some reason they thought I would be suitable. I politely explained that I would be the wrong person for that job as I was sure that there would be plenty of other people in Cardiff more suitable for it. I explained that even though I felt very honoured to be considered, I had to be honest that I wouldn't be able to do the job.

After some persuasion and much deliberation, I decided to take the role. I remember going with Darren to one of the major bookshops in Cardiff and buying a book on accountancy – as if that was going to help me! I couldn't understand a word of it. On my first day I remember thinking, who do I think I am, doing this? I felt sorry for the charity as I wondered at what moment they would realize they had made a huge mistake and had wasted their time trying to train me.

Despite my relationship with numbers, I was surprised that I did do an OK job. I actually liked making budgets work and learning how to set aside monies. Although I loved the organization and what they did, it wasn't my ideal role, but God taught me something through my time there that has stayed with me for the rest of my life. I was the most unlikely of people to do that job but God was starting to show me not to limit him. Whenever he asks you to do something, if he calls you to it, he will equip you. Again, just like those we read about in the Bible, he uses the unexpected and the unlikeliest.

In Scripture it reminds us that God can do anything! 'God can do anything, you know – far more than you could ever imagine or guess or request in your wildest dreams!' (Eph. 3:20, MSG).

One particular role I was offered was like a dream job working for a television channel. I remember that first day they took me to pick up my new car that would be needed for the role. Anything I needed for that role they would provide for me. I couldn't believe I was given this amazing opportunity. However, as I went back to my hotel that first night of training I knew that although this was exciting, it was the wrong path for me. Trying to explain why was difficult as I didn't really know myself. I'm sure they thought I was crazy but I knew there and then that I had to make the right decision and leave even if I didn't quite understand it at the time.

When we ask God to be Lord of our lives that means that we need to trust him even when things don't make sense. If we are putting God in the centre of our choices and decisions then sometimes we need to step away from all that looks appealing and exciting to hear that still small voice. Sometimes we will hear the word 'no'.

As a parent, telling a child they cannot do or have something, is not easy – especially if that thing brings enjoyment for the child. We as parents can see why that 'no' is for their own good and said out of love or protection, but it can be hard if the child doesn't understand that.

I used to feel so cruel when my little dog wanted the food I was eating. Some of the healthy foods I could share, but I couldn't share any chocolate or sweet treats as they would be harmful to her. I remember her little face looking at me, smelling the sweet aromas, almost pleading with me with her eyes to give her some. I couldn't explain to a dog why but my actions were to protect her, even if she didn't realize it.

Hearing the word 'no' is not always a bad thing. God knows what is best for us and for others. Even though I thought that television channel role was an amazing opportunity, I knew it wasn't right for me. After I stepped aside I'm sure the organization filled it with exactly the right person for it.

Sometimes, if we ignore God's direction for us, it can take us a whole lot longer to get back on the right track. God knows the plans and paths for us and I had learned that listening to the voice of the Spirit at every stage of our lives is important.

Sometimes people will not understand the decisions we make and think we are crazy, but that is OK. They have their journeys and we must be accountable for our own.

To this day, when I see on the road the car that was given to me that first day of my new role, I have a selfish pang of disappointment, but I know I had made the right decision. Our journey in life can come with its frustrations, sacrifices and hardships and we can learn life lessons through these times but we can also experience many blessings, breakthroughs and miracles along the way too.

I once had an idea of reaching out to the women in the community. We wanted to bridge the gap between the church and the people, and to connect with those around us, so I planned a local event for women. It wasn't necessarily going to be held in the church but somewhere in Bridgend that local women would quite happily come to.

I had negotiated with a hotel in Bridgend to hire a large room for the evening and the idea was to fill it with all things most women love under one roof. I went around all the shops in the area that women loved to shop in and talked to their staff about a huge event that was happening and how they needed to be a part of it by having a stall to sell some of their products. I didn't have a clue how this was going to go and whether anyone would even come to it but I was so sure this idea was God-given. It could have been a complete disaster but I felt led to go with what God was showing me. I was learning that my confidence was now in him, not in my abilities.

With a small team from church, we secured about twenty-five mini pop-up stalls from all our favourite shops and we had an area filled with beauty-pampering stations from local businesses. The money raised from the event all went to supporting local charities or mission work. These events weren't a trick to get women to church but more of a way of getting women together and connecting with them. To my relief many tickets were sold and many women and local businesses seemed to love it.

At that time, there was nothing like these events around and so they soon became quite popular with not only the local people but with women living further afield. We ended up organizing two of these events every year – one in the summer and one at Christmas. We soon outgrew the hotel and ended up holding our last one at the theatre in Porthcawl.

The events didn't necessarily grow the church overnight but it enabled us to connect with the community and build relationships with not only the women but also local businesses. People became more familiar with the church and got to know us. Personally, it also gave me lots of experience in event management which was completely new to me, but even that was all part of God's plan for what was ahead.

I loved watching this little idea grow into something so much more than what I initially dreamed of. Making it happen with no budget, then seeing what it became, taught me a valuable lesson of learning again that God can do so much through us if we trust in what he is telling us to do. I could have so easily thought the idea was ridiculous but when an idea is from God, so much can come from stepping out in faith and watch his hands at work.

Looking back, God was teaching me about how mighty his hands were even back then – it was something that was being ingrained in me and this was key for me in how I navigated the health journey that was ahead of me. There was, however, even more he wanted to teach me in the years that followed.

In 2009 while we were still leading the church in Bridgend, I was asked to join the Aspire team by the wife of the then general superintendent, Marilyn Glass, who founded and led the ministry. Aspire was Elim's national women's ministry with the aim of encouraging women to rise up and be all that God created them to be. I loved the heart and vision of the ministry and, through regional and national conferences, and supporting local churches, many women were reached and inspired. I was so excited to be given this opportunity and I realized that the experience I had running those women's events in Bridgend would really help me in organizing regional conferences for the ministry. I could see how God had prepared me for this next season of reaching women.

In 2016 I was offered the role of leading Aspire by Elim's National Leadership Team. Talking about how God asks the unexpected to do his exploits, it was definitely one of those moments. I was completely and utterly surprised and felt very humbled by the opportunity. I felt this role was really going to push me out of my comfort zone even further and I remember describing it as being given a jumper that was far too big on me. I wondered how on earth I would stand on platforms and speak to hundreds of women and sit in boardrooms with other leaders. However, the lessons I had learned prior to this had led me to believe that when opportunities came my way, I had to believe that God would equip me and the fact he believed in me is what mattered. God had called me to lead this ministry for a season and a purpose and I wanted to be obedient yet again to that call.

During the last six years of leading Aspire, I have seen God at work in the lives of so many women. Women of all ages accomplishing things that they never dreamed possible has been truly inspiring for all of us on the team to see. The ministry has not only reached many women in the UK but it continues to reach women globally too.

Having the opportunity to lead this ministry alongside an incredible team of women has taught me not only about leadership, but also how important it is to know that it's all about serving God and others. I still have moments of feeling totally under-qualified but I have come to like 'oversized jumpers' as, even though they can initially feel uncomfortable, the fact that they are too big means there is so much growing and learning to experience. My ability to do so always comes from God and I have valued and cherished this opportunity to serve him and the women in our churches.

Going back to those initial days of leading Aspire – I remember one of my first speaking engagements in my new role was at the Aspire regional conference at City Gates Church, Ilford. There were around four hundred women attending that day and the other guest speaker was Jen Baker who was a very accomplished speaker and communicator. Jen was the first session speaker and I was due to follow her in the second session. If that wasn't enough pressure, I grabbed my bottle of water for a drink just before I went up to speak. As I put it to the side of me, I soon felt a warmish, wet feeling on my lap. I looked down, only to see that my water bottle had fallen to one side and started to pump water all over the front of my jeans. It really did look as though I had had an accident! There was no time to rush to the toilets and dry this off so I had to walk up to the platform and stand there being introduced as the new leader of Aspire – with a huge wet patch!

I did see the funny side and quickly brought attention to it to avoid any raised eyebrows and whispers from the congregation . . . but looking back, I felt it taught me some-thing right at the start of my journey in the leadership role. I was putting high expectations on myself about how I needed to be. I was aware of the big shoes I was filling and I was probably entertaining some thoughts of doubt as to whether I was able to fulfil the role. I had even been wondering whether my outfit was the right choice and how I was going to follow such an experienced gifted speaker, probably overthinking far too many things that day. But there I was, standing in front of everyone soaking wet and I guess it broke something in me right at the start. Being so nervous initially and doubting my ability, I had to remember it was never about me anyway. It was all about God, so why was I worrying whether or not I could do it? I needed to be real, authentic and to be myself. I needed to do what God was calling me to do and my eyes needed only to be on him. If he had opened doors of oppor-tunities for me to tell others about him, then surely he would equip me?

We moved from Bridgend to Salisbury in 2011 as Darren was offered the senior pastor role at the Elim church there. Moving away from Wales was a big step for me. I had loved living there and this was where most of my family lived. How-ever, I knew the move would develop Darren further in lead-ership and I knew if we wanted all that God had for us we needed to take this opportunity. Alongside the Aspire role, I was involved in helping Darren lead the Elim church in Salisbury and again we learned many lessons in leadership in this place and were grateful for the opportunity to grow in ministry.

Six years later we moved to Hereford where Darren took up a new role as the senior pastor of Hereford Elim. I continued to lead Aspire and also worked at Elim International Centre in an administration role during the week.

Over the next few years I was learning to recognize the voice of the Holy Spirit. I had watched others giving people encouraging words from the Lord but didn't realize that God could use me in this way too. I had been on the receiving end of such words and knew the impact they had had in my own life. Sharing what I felt the Holy Spirit show me for someone else pushed me again out of my comfort zone as it meant being bold and speaking out. God was gently taking me by the hand and teaching me about listening to his voice.

In the book of Isaiah it tells us that God's ways are far higher than ours: 'For my thoughts are not your thoughts, neither are your ways my ways,' declares the LORD. 'As the heavens are higher than the earth, so are my ways higher than your ways and my thoughts than your thoughts' (Isa. 55:8–9, NIV). This verse has become a favourite of mine as, each time I read it, it reminds me that when I think I can't do something or if a situation seems impossible, God has other ideas and ways so we just need to trust and believe that he has the best plan. We often try to work out how a prayer can be answered, and when we can't think how it can be possible, we lose faith in the outcome. However, God's ways and thoughts are far higher than ours, so we should stop imposing our own limits on him.

In God's word it also reminds us that we should trust him and not rely on our own understanding:

Trust in the LORD with all your heart,
    and do not lean on your own understanding.
In all your ways acknowledge him,
    and he will make straight your paths.

(Prov. 3:5–6, ESV)

As I love to organize, get structures in place and plan ahead, I have come to realize that in some situations, where my tendency is to have it all worked out and a plan firmly in place, I need to stop, and leave it in God's hands. His ways of working things out are far better than mine and the way he does it continues to amaze me. Being on the journey of learning to hear the voice of God has meant pushing through the fear of being bold and doing what he asks me to do. This wasn't easy for me, but it was something I really desired to be obedient in. I guess I was more passionate about being obedient and experiencing what he could do through me than feeling nervous or being too shy. Hearing God and being used by him to speak to people, and then seeing them encouraged by him, is something that fills me with joy.

In the Gospel of John it talks about how Jesus came to give us life, but not just life – a full life! I have learned that following Jesus and his ways is actually not only a life of fulfilment but a life full of adventure.

I'm not sure if those nerves will ever go as I step 'out of my plane' onto a platform to speak and, to this day, my default is always to swerve those opportunities or push others out there instead of me. However, what I have learned is even though it's OK to be happy with the behind-the-scenes stuff (and that is my comfortable place!) stepping out of my comfort zone, makes me more reliant on Jesus.

Obeying the Lord and doing what he is calling me to do, is fulfilling and purposeful. Seeing him work through me in ways that I never have dreamed possible spurs me on to be more available for him. It is a journey on which I have walked hand in hand with Jesus and even today, he continues to pull me gently from behind the wall.

When Moses had led the Israelites out of Egypt on a forty-year journey through the wilderness, they came to Mount Horeb where they set up camp. They were situated just across the Jordan River from the promised land in Canaan and they were positioned ready to take the land. However, life at Mount Horeb was rather pleasant for them. They were fed by the Lord, their clothes and possessions didn't wear out, they had rest from their travels and the Lord provided a covering from the heat during the day and a pillar of fire to warm them at night. They had stayed there for two years – life was good!

However, we read in the story that God tells them to move on: 'The LORD our God said to us at Horeb, "You have stayed long enough at this mountain. Break camp and advance . . ."' (Deut. 1:6–7a, NIV). Mount Horeb was a transitional place where they had received instruction and even though life was good there, God hadn't brought them out of Egypt to stay there. His plan for them was to enter the promised land so, even though they were comfortable, they needed now to advance.

Looking back to the early years when Darren was training for ministry (and I was saying 'no' to every opportunity), I could easily have stayed in my comfort zone. It was the same when God called us to new places to live and minister. When we used to consider a move and what it took to move house, to settle the kids in new schools, to make new friends, to move away from family and all that we knew and were comfortable with, it was so tempting to stay put. We don't always see what God has for us in another place. Settling for 'comfortable' can seem so much easier.

I have learned that God gives us a choice. He never forces us to do anything and he will still bless us wherever we are.

However, sometimes to experience all that God wants to do in and through us, he can call us to a different place. That place can become your connection to where God wants to take you next. Stepping into the unknown or into roles that you think you can't do takes courage, it takes effort. Those initial steps are 'uncomfortable'.

## His Hands

The way Jesus took hold of my hand and led me from behind the wall in life is something that I can only describe as 'gentle'. When we read that well-known passage in Psalm 23 it is a description of how the Lord not only goes before us and prepares the way, but also gently leads and guides us.

> The Lord is my shepherd, I lack nothing.
>     He makes me lie down in green pastures,
> he leads me beside quiet waters,
>     he refreshes my soul.
> He guides me along the right paths
>     for his name's sake.
> Even though I walk
>     through the darkest valley,
> I will fear no evil,
>     for you are with me;
> your rod and your staff,
>     they comfort me.
> You prepare a table before me
>     in the presence of my enemies.

You anoint my head with oil;
    my cup overflows.
Surely your goodness and love will follow me
    all the days of my life,
and I will dwell in the house of the Lord
    for ever.

(Ps. 23:1–6, NIV)

This passage of Scripture is a reminder that goodness and love will follow us on our journey and will comfort and refresh us when needed.

Going back to the verse in Ephesians where it reminds us that God can do anything, the second part tells us how he does it: 'God can do anything, you know – far more than you could ever imagine or guess or request in your wildest dreams! He does it not by pushing us around but by working within us, his Spirit deeply and gently within us' (Eph. 3:20, MSG).

God's hands gently led me from behind a wall, out of hiding. His hands gently led me to jobs that I thought were far above my capability. His hands gently pushed me out of my comfort zone on numerous occasions. His hands gently pulled me away from things that weren't for me. I was learning that yes, his hands are strong and mighty, but they are gentle hands too. I was learning that when God holds out his hands, like a father does to his child, I can trust them.

God's hands guide us and put us on the right paths in life. However, as previously mentioned, we need to listen to his voice along the journey to make sure we keep on the right path. Sometimes we think we know better and take paths of our own and then we end up far away from where we are meant to be.

It is like going on a journey in your car and putting on the sat nav. You punch in the postcode and sometimes it gives you the option for the fastest route. That route isn't always the most familiar or the one you would necessarily choose – but the sat nav works out the fastest route based on the delays ahead that day. There have been numerous times that I have ignored the fastest route given as I have been so convinced my way of getting there was the fastest, only then to be faced with annoying roadblocks and diversions. There have been times when I have even muted the spoken instructions and put on some music instead, only to miss the slip road off a motorway. Those journeys have often left me very frustrated, not to mention very late.

Sometimes we think we are making the right choices even though we sense the Holy Spirit is telling us otherwise. It's as though we put on the mute button over his voice because we don't want to hear it. Listening to the Holy Spirit is vital for our journeys and for keeping on the right path. We can all gravitate to what feels good or get tempted by what looks attractive, but God's word tells us why we should listen to his voice and take heed of his instruction:

Listen, my son, accept what I say,
    and the years of your life will be many.
I instruct you in the way of wisdom
    and lead you along straight paths.
When you walk, your steps will not be hampered;
    when you run, you will not stumble.
Hold on to instruction, do not let it go;
    guard it well, for it is your life.
Do not set foot on the path of the wicked
    or walk in the way of evildoers.

Avoid it, do not travel on it;
   turn from it and go on your way.

(Prov. 4:10–15, NIV)

I love seeing a potter at the wheel making something from a piece of clay. What seems to be a useless mound of grey mud soon gets moulded into a useful pot or beautiful ornament. There is much time spent creating that vessel and the potter is very careful to get it just right – fit for its purpose. Looking back at my early years in ministry, I can see how God brought situations across my path to mould me into the person he had created me to be and I am still being moulded today – I am definitely not the finished product! You see, so often we see ourselves as that lump of clay and have no idea what is about to be created, but just as the potter knows what he is making, God already knows what he can create from your life. If you only knew what he had in store for you. We need to allow his hands to continually mould and shape us and be available to be used as vessels for him.

Yet you, LORD, are our Father.
   We are the clay, you are the potter;
   we are all the work of your hand.

(Isa. 64:8, NIV)

Thinking about the hands of God – his hands not only mould us but often knit 'baggy jumpers' for us all to wear. Opportunities can come across our paths that we feel very unequipped for but we need to remember that, although those baggy jumpers or shoes seem too big they are often just the right size. It is in our weakness that he is strong.

But he said to me, 'My grace is sufficient for you, for my power is made perfect in weakness.' Therefore I will boast all the more gladly about my weaknesses, so that Christ's power may rest on me. That is why, for Christ's sake, I delight in weaknesses, in insults, in hardships, in persecutions, in difficulties. For when I am weak, then I am strong.

(2 Cor. 12:9–10, NIV)

## Take a Moment . . .

Have you ever felt God prompting you to dream big?

Have there been ideas given to you by God that you are still sitting on?

Have you excluded yourself from jobs and roles because you think that you are not capable?

Maybe you have become too comfortable right now and God is waiting for you to advance into something new. Bring these things to God afresh again today.

With his hands he is creating a beautiful vessel out of your life so allow him to shape, mould and refine you.

Remember we don't always know the direction in which he is taking us so be patient in the creating process . . . And if you need to wear a baggy jumper for a while, know his hands have created it perfectly for you.

# 4

# The Gift Tag

It was 11 December 2020, and we had arrived at the Nuffield Hospital in Cheltenham where I was about to find out what the lump in my breast was. Darren was allowed in the waiting area with me and, even though I was too nervous to talk, just having him there was a comfort. There was a woman opposite me who was also with her husband. She too looked nervous and I could tell she was probably there for the same reason as me and my heart went out to her. I tried to make eye contact with her. I wanted to give her a reassuring look, a look like to show I knew what she was going through, a look to say, 'It's OK' but her head was down and I understood. As I sat there I looked through the Bible verses on my phone that had been filling me with comfort during the past few days – verses telling me to be strong and verses reminding me not to fear.

The lady who was opposite was called to see the consultant just before I was called to have a mammogram. After the mammogram, I sat back out in the waiting room, ready for the consultant to call me through. I saw the woman who had gone in before me just leaving with her husband. She was chatty, laughing with the receptionist – she looked relieved and different. I could tell it was probably good news. I was so relieved for her and it gave me hope that I too would be leaving in the same way.

The consultant called my name. He was bright, cheery and had an excellent manner with his patients. There was a lovely nurse with him. He explained that he was going to give me an ultrasound scan. As I lay down for the scan I was scared. I knew I would discover what this was and my life could change.

The nurse came round to the other side of me and both she and the consultant were explaining everything so clearly. As he started to scan me, the talking stopped. The consultant went quiet as he concentrated hard, looking at the screen. I was waiting for him to say it was all OK but there was a silence that seemed to last forever. After he had finished scanning me he explained he needed to take a biopsy of the lump. This was something that I knew could happen even if it wasn't cancer so I still wasn't too sure of the outcome.

As he left the room to get equipment, the nurse grabbed my hand and told me that the area did look suspicious but just encouraged me that I was doing well. As I was lying there, I looked up at the ceiling and everything seemed surreal. The consultant explained that my lymph nodes seemed OK but there was one that he wasn't too sure of so he needed to take some samples of that too. The biopsies were taken as the nurse held my hand. This wasn't what I was expecting. I couldn't cry, I just went along with whatever they needed to do. As I got dressed the consultant told me to get Darren and to come through to his office when we were ready.

As I walked back out into the waiting room, Darren looked up at me. I remember his eyes were looking for me to say that everything was OK again. I shook my head and asked him to come with me. I grabbed his hand as we went towards the consultant's office. I held it tight as I told him it wasn't good news and we both walked down the corridor feeling stunned. We sat in the office and the consultant explained that yes, I did have breast cancer, but the good news was that it was in the early stages. He thought the tumour was around two centimetres although this would be clarified later on. He didn't think it had gone to my lymph nodes but there was one lymph node they needed to check to make sure. The consultant still seemed bright and confident and this put me at ease.

He explained I would need chemo and I remember Darren asking a few questions.

As my father's mother had had cancer in her fallopian tubes and his sister had breast cancer, there was a high possibility this cancer could be genetic and this would need checking, but the next stage was to see what type of cancer I had. They would then know what type of treatment I would need. Therefore, an appointment was given for a week later when the results would be back.

I had held in my tears until I left the hospital. As we walked to the car, I couldn't stop the sobs and I desperately needed to get in the car to let them out. As we sat in the car, I think the first thing I said as I was sobbing was, 'I am going to be bald for Abi's wedding.' My daughter Abi was due to get married the following September. Looking back, I don't know why that was the thing that came to me first but I think it just hit me that the next few months – months that were meant to be full of excitement in planning my daughter's wedding – suddenly had changed.

I guess one of the first feelings I felt, apart from fear of the unknown in that moment, was that of disappointment. We were in the middle of a pandemic and already many were facing numerous disappointments. It was almost as if we were becoming a nation that was getting used to feeling disappointed. Many people had to cancel and change plans only to cancel and change them repeatedly. Holidays, events, concerts, weddings, lockdowns, release dates were all being cancelled and new dates being set all the time. Even my own niece had cancelled her wedding plans a few times that year. Nobody could seem to plan anything and this caused disappointment for so many.

When we think about the word 'disappointment' and what that means, we think of that feeling when someone has let you down or something that wasn't as good as what you thought it would be. I have also heard it described as feeling 'defeated in hope'. I think in that moment that's exactly how I felt. Besides the uncertainty of the unknown and the fear that went with that, I felt 'defeated' in all the plans I had for that year and for the immediate future.

For months, I had planned the lead-up to my daughter's wedding with her. We had made plans for us to go wedding shopping, plans on what to do for her bridal shower, plans to go to the hairdresser's – we had been planning outfits and outings for months. I wanted to share this special lead-up with her, as any mum would have dreamed about. Suddenly, I realized this would look very different now. I would soon lose my hair, I would have to isolate more due to the treatment, and would I even be well enough to enjoy any of the lead-up that I dreamed about for so long with her? I felt disappointment at such a deep level in those moments. This wasn't how it was meant to be and for somebody that likes to plan and fix things, I couldn't change or fix this.

I didn't want my family upset or to be worrying about me and that day telling everyone was hard. There was a huge comfort that the cancer had been caught early and we were all so grateful for that but getting my head around it all was something I needed to adjust to. I found myself trying to reassure everyone as the thought of them worrying about me just upset me so much.

The following week was a blur to me. Christmas was only two weeks away so I decided to try to keep busy with wrapping presents. How was I going to get through Christmas? A time when there is joy and excitement. A time when families get together and have fun. I had to film Christmas video greetings for Aspire and church and the thought of standing there with tinsel in my hair trying to be festive and joyous was something I felt I couldn't face. How was I going to keep it normal for my family? My results were in a week and I knew that week I needed to occupy myself.

I had lovely Christmas boxes for each of my family. I put lots of presents in each one for them. As I was wrapping them and placing them in their boxes, I felt God asking me what I wanted for Christmas too. I felt he was telling me to write it down and put it in a Christmas box. I grabbed the nearest gift tag and on it I wrote three things.

1.  For the best outcome (that the treatment would work).
2.  Easy (meaning treatment would be straightforward).
3.  That the cancer hadn't gone to my lymph nodes.

I signed it, 'Love, Father'. Almost as though, if I wanted a gift from him this Christmas, this would be it.

I placed the tag in the box. This was the start of a faith journey with God. I had spoken and preached about having faith in God so many times and now I was at a point where everything I preached about, I needed to live out for myself. There had been times when I had seen God's hands in action, and times he had taught me to have faith in him. I had so much faith for others when I used to pray for them, but now I needed to have that very same faith for myself.

I returned to the hospital the following week and was told that the cancer was a triple negative type and a grade three. It was hard taking everything in as I didn't know initially what all this meant. I learned that this was an aggressive cancer (and most likely caused by the altered BRCA 1 gene) but the good news was it hadn't gone to my lymph nodes. God had heard and answered one of my gift tag requests.

## His Hands

Going back to that favourite verse of mine in Isaiah, where God tells us that his thoughts and ways are far better than ours, I have learned that when we are feeling disappointed, often we learn down the line that God brings about an even better plan. When I look back now at those things I felt initially disappointed about, God actually made those times even more special. Despite our plans not going the way we thought, he made other moments even better than what I imagined. My outlook on life changed considerably during my cancer journey and when I look back at those so-called initial disappointments, I do become a little embarrassed that I felt so disappointed about such things in light of my diagnosis.

One of the major things I learned on this journey is we can overcome disappointment – and we do that by replacing it with thankfulness. It is OK to feel the emotion of disappointment because, as I said earlier, we are human. However, what we do with disappointment is key to how it affects us going forward. When we feel 'defeated in hope' in one thing there are surely at least ten other things we can be thankful about.

When I started to put things in perspective, I became so thankful that I was even alive to share in my daughter's wedding plans that those initial disappointments became insignificant. Having name places and wedding favours to make and helping her look for bridesmaids' dresses all from my sofa were huge distractions through my treatment. For a person who loves organizing events, a daughter's wedding is the ultimate. It gave me a focus and lots of enjoyable things to do during the darkest times of my treatment, especially when I couldn't go anywhere.

Even though I initially felt disappointed at the timing of this diagnosis, I thank God that I had the time to plan a wedding with my daughter and her fiancé Luke. The lead-up actually made me more grateful for this special time in my daughter's life and all the creative touches that were prepared for the day were made with so much more love and attention.

What I would wear to her bridal shower seemed irrelevant as time went on. I was thankful that my daughter had found someone to share her life with. I look back at the pictures of her bridal shower and there I was in a baggy t-shirt and cap – so far from my plans, but I was so happy to be there with her for that occasion in her life.

Those things I was disappointed in didn't matter at all. I was thankful that we were able to give her a wedding that was shared with all our nearest and dearest and that I was able to be present. It could have been so different. My outlook had changed. Yes, there was a natural disappointment I wasn't with her the day she found 'the' wedding dress, but I was so thankful I could be there by Zoom and technology enabled that. I was thankful that my parents had the joy of being with her that day. It is something that I am sure they will never forget and, for that, I am thankful.

There was an old song that I heard in church when I was young about counting your blessings. The words went on to say that as you count them you'd be surprised at what God has done. When you turn disappointments, however big they are, into thankfulness, it shifts your focus. Instead of focusing on what you haven't got, it makes you focus on all the good that you actually do have in life and it makes you realize what you are actually blessed with.

The Bible reminds us to give thanks in *all* circumstances – so that's not just giving thanks when things are good: 'Give thanks in all circumstances; for this is God's will for you in Christ Jesus' (1 Thess. 5:18, NIV).

With his hands, God created moments for me in the lead-up to Abi's wedding that I probably wouldn't have had time for had I been working. I shared these times not only with my daughter but with my mum too and we were all together making those precious memories. He turned my 'defeated in hope' into feeling that I was actually so incredibly blessed.

**Take a Moment . . .**

We have all experienced disappointments in life. Ask yourself today, what am I disappointed about?

Have people let you down? Has life not turned out as expected?

We can easily carry around those disappointments for years and, if we allow it, they can stop us moving forward.

Why not hand those disappointments to Jesus right now and, as you do, make a list of at least ten things today that you are thankful to him for?

Focus on all the blessings in your life that you do have and, as you do – let those other disappointments go!

# 5

# The Dot

Christmas 2020 was difficult. Although we still spent it all together as a family, it was hard to fully enjoy the season. I didn't want people feeling sad for me around a happy time of year and so, apart from close family and friends, I hadn't told many people about my diagnosis. I tried to keep things as normal as possible but inside there was still much uncertainty. I love Christmas-time but that year I almost wanted the season to pass quickly so I could start a new year afresh and begin my treatment.

One evening after Christmas before my treatment had started, Abi and I sat downstairs and worshipped. It was a powerful time and we sensed the presence of God in the lounge. We later called Darren and Jack in to join us to pray. We just felt as a family we needed to give all this to God at the start of my treatment.

My first appointment with my oncologist and breast surgeon was on 31 December. I remember that day so well. Although I always appreciated hospitals and the NHS staff, I was quite anxious whenever I walked into a hospital, even if it was simply to visit people. Being part of a large wider family, I visited many sick relatives in hospital while I was growing up. Some of my uncles, aunties and grandparents fought awful illnesses and so I think my experience of hospitals as a child was filled with sadness, shock and bad news.

Walking into the cancer unit at Hereford Hospital that day, I was feeling so nervous. Due to Covid-19, I had a mask and a visor on and as soon as I went through the doors, my temperature was taken and I was asked lots of questions. This was the general procedure for walking into a hospital during this time. There was a fear of Covid-19 everywhere and people were sat meters apart with seats being constantly wiped down.

You couldn't take anyone with you into hospital during the pandemic so I sat in the waiting room on my own. No one chatted with each other out of fear of catching Covid-19 – especially in a cancer unit where you needed to be extra careful. With that general fear around on top of the uncertainty of what I was facing, I was frozen to my chair as I looked at all the other patients around me.

I couldn't believe I was sitting in a cancer unit waiting room to see an oncologist and breast surgeon about the treatment ahead. I had a diagnosis that I had feared so much during my early life but I held on to the verse in Isaiah that I felt God had led me to right at the start, telling me not to fear and that he would strengthen me. Isaiah 41:10 was engraved around my neck, almost literally. I had had the Scripture reference engraved on a heart pendant and I wore it around my neck throughout my treatment as a reminder of God's promises. Yes, I was scared, but I knew he was steadying me and giving me strength to face this with his mighty hands.

I met my oncologist, who seemed a nice, gentle man. I had conjured up an image of him that would be serious, matter-of-fact and cold but he was actually the opposite. He took me through my treatment plan and told me that my lump was just over 3.5cms, so a bit bigger than originally thought. I sat there and listened but just wanted the appointment to go quickly. The new information that the tumour seemed bigger than expected was enough. I didn't want any new information that was going to shock me so I didn't ask many questions.

I had decided early on that the way I was going to deal with this was *not* to go on the internet and search my type of cancer. While the nurse at Cheltenham Hospital was giving me all the leaflets and information on breast cancer, she had turned around and told me not to believe everything I would come across on the internet regarding the triple negative type of cancer. She told me she had plenty of patients who had come through it. I didn't know at the time whether she knew that an internet search for the type of cancer I had would produce all sorts of negative articles or if it was just a general piece of advice for my own good. However, not searching about it was something I decided upon from the start. I didn't want to go on forums and search websites as I didn't want to fill my head with possible bad experiences. I knew that every piece of negative information would stick to me like glue. I realized there were many positive, encouraging stories out there that could inspire me and give me hope, but I knew I would stumble across the opposite too. I wanted to keep fear away from me so I decided to listen to those who were taking care of me and totally to keep my eyes on Jesus through this.

I realize that some find the support of a wider network helpful. I knew of people who needed every bit of information and would want to look into a subject more and find out everything they could – I understand how that could be helpful. However, for myself, I needed to push fear away as much as I could, so I decided to 'guard my heart' and limit what I allowed in.

After the appointment with my oncologist, I was taken through to see a breast nurse. She too gave me lots of information and took me through the contents of a folder. I don't think I was taking much in at this point as it all became a bit surreal and what was actually happening seemed to hit me. As she shared the basic information, I could feel myself starting to get overwhelmed. I had been so strong up until this point but as the realization of what was happening started to kick in,

I began to cry. As soon as the nurse started handing me tissues, the breast surgeon called me through. There was no time to cry so I got myself together and went through to his office.

As the breast surgeon looked at my scan on his screen, he pointed out that the radiologist had flagged up another 'suspicious area' on the scan. It was not far from the initial tumour. The advice was that this area needed looking at in detail by a radiologist consultant. By now, I was feeling that it was all becoming too much for me. I needed Darren there with me to ask the questions that I couldn't.

As the breast surgeon scanned me and made his notes, he also inserted a marker peg inside me, into the tumour. As the chemo would hopefully shrink the tumour they needed to make sure they knew where the area was. Even though I hated hospitals I used to be quite brave and strong in procedures – it's almost as if my fears were always about the unknown. The marker was inserted and I was ready to leave with an appointment for 5 January when I would have another ultrasound regarding the 'suspicious area'.

My parents had come to stay with us during my treatment and it was always so comforting that whenever I came home from any appointment with Darren, they would be there with a cup of tea ready and something that my Mum had baked. That day I sat down with the welcome hot drink, feeling totally overwhelmed. To deal now with another possible area was almost too much. I couldn't read all the information and folders that they had given me so I put them in a pile for 'another day'. I felt I wanted to hibernate from this nightmare.

However, there was something within that always seemed to stop me from going to the worst-case scenario. It was actually the opposite of how I have usually handled health fears throughout my life. Despite my natural, human feelings, I did trust that God was with me, I felt his presence with me and it was as if his hands were shielding my heart.

My chemo was scheduled to start on 11 January but before that, I needed the extra ultrasound appointment and an MRI. The breast surgeon wanted an MRI at the start of the treatment and then one at the end, so the first MRI scan was scheduled in Cheltenham the day after my ultrasound scan. Again, I needed to face the fears of the unknown and the words 'be strong' kept coming back to me.

The night before the ultrasound scan, I was in the house on my own. My parents had gone home for a few days before returning for my chemo. Darren and Jack had gone to the gym and Abi had gone back to visit her fiancé, Luke. I felt I needed this time on my own with God. I cried out to him and prayed that if that area was something sinister God would change the picture. The Scripture in Matthew's Gospel where it talks about having that mustard seed size faith was in my mind: 'He replied, "Because you have so little faith. Truly I tell you, if you have faith as small as a mustard seed, you can say to this mountain, 'Move from here to there,' and it will move. Nothing will be impossible for you"' (Matt. 17:20, NIV). I had faith larger than a mustard seed in that moment. So, with the ultrasound scan booked for the following morning, I believed that God would change the picture.

The next day I sat in the waiting room waiting for my ultrasound scan. Abi was messaging me on my phone and she sent me a dot. It became our reminder to each other, something we would text back and forth throughout my treatment, that we just needed a mustard seed-sized faith for God to move mountains. God had spoken to us back in October about mountains and I knew this was significant for me in this season. I had a mustard seed-like dot of faith in those moments.

I walked into the scanning room with confidence that God could change the picture there and then. I lay down on the bed and the consultant radiologist scanned me. As she scanned the area, she told me very quickly that the area was nothing more than an innocent lymph node and it was nothing to worry about.

I believe that, if that area had been something sinister previously, God changed the picture that day and, if it was an innocent node all along, he was teaching me so much about walking in that level of faith. I came away thanking him. He had heard my prayer and had seen the dot of faith.

## His Hands

The day of the journey to Cardiff in October before my diagnosis had been significant for me. I had known God was showing me something that day but had no idea it was going to relate to what was to come. The video I took on my phone of what seemed like a mountain reducing in front of us is the only way I can describe what happened to me many times on this journey – that I would be faced with a mountain, something that seemed impossible to move, but I saw it being removed before my eyes. I believed that through treatment God could reduce the tumour and heal me.

When I began praying about the other 'suspicious area', I think everything within me was saying 'no' to accepting it. There are times when we need to stand up, shout a loud 'no' to the devil, and declare what the word of God says over our lives: 'So let God work his will in you. Yell a loud no to the Devil and watch him make himself scarce' (Jas 4:7, MSG).

I know there may be many reading this who, like me, have prayed earnestly for loved ones to be healed and that healing didn't happen. There have been many faith-filled believers who have had the faith that God could heal them but they were taken home earlier than expected or wanted. I will be honest and admit that I don't know why some people are healed and others are not. I don't have many of the answers to those questions, although there are many books written on this subject.

All I know is that God loves us all the same and doesn't have favourites – it says so in his word: 'For God does not show favouritism' (Rom. 2:11, NIV). What I do know is that there is a time and season for everything:

> There is a time for everything,
>> and a season for every activity under the heavens:
>> a time to be born and a time to die,
>> a time to plant and a time to uproot.

(Eccl. 3:1–2, NIV)

The chapter states there is an appointed time for things to happen and, although we may not fully understand the timings of these things, God knows the beginning from the end and our lives are in his hands. We are all going to leave this earth at some point, and that is certain; however, none of us know when that will be – only God knows that. Even though we don't know when our time will end here on this earth, it's important for us to know that God can heal today and if it's his will, it will be done. We have to operate in that level of faith.

**Take a Moment . . .**

What situation in your life just needs dot-sized faith that God can change things?

That job situation, that relationship, that sickness, that financial need, that family situation, those things that perhaps you haven't even prayed about before or for a long time as you have already classed them as 'unchangeable'?

Sometimes we need to rise up, yell a loud 'no' to the devil and trample on the lie that these things are not moveable.

Declare victory over that thing right now in the name of Jesus and believe he can paint a new picture with his hands.

# 6

# Heart Guard

I mentioned in the previous chapter the importance of 'guarding my heart' during this season. The heart matters! When I was given the role of leading Aspire I had a few people giving me some words of wisdom as I took this leadership position. The advice was that I should 'guard my heart' and I guess it was given as just a general piece of advice for any leader.

One day, around that same time, I was waiting in a pharmacy with Abi for a prescription and we started to talk to an elderly lady who was also waiting for her medication. We chatted away and ended up giving her a lift into town as she was going in our direction. It was as though we had known her for years but as she left the car she turned to us and said something along the lines of 'and don't forget to guard your heart'. As I had already heard this bit of advice a couple of weeks earlier, it made me sit up and take more notice of it, especially when it was given from a complete stranger. Over the years, I have seen why this piece of advice was so important to me for numerous reasons.

If we think about the heart as an organ, its purpose is to pump blood around our body so that we can live. Without this organ we cannot survive, so it is an important part of our body. If the heart is faulty or not working as it should, it can affect our whole body.

We all know the importance of looking after our hearts in what we eat and how much exercise we do. However, one verse in Scripture talks about the heart as being the very essence of who we are: the way we think, our actions, our motives, our responses, our conversations. It is those things that need guarding. This verse clearly suggests we need to guard those things because the heart shapes who we are, what happens next and the direction in which we are going.

Above all else, guard your heart,
for everything you do flows from it.

(Prov. 4:23, NIV)

How we respond to situations is important for keeping our 'hearts' (us) healthy. Things like rejection, offence and betrayal can hurt us and divert us from our paths if we allow it. It's easy to want to throw in the towel when we are hit with some of these things and so making sure we guard how we respond is key. The steps we make from that place are vital in keeping us 'healthy'. We have a choice either to stay offended or to choose to forgive, to let go and keep moving on.

I knew I had to guard my heart and what I allowed into it during my health battle. Yes, I had to be real about the possibilities of the outcome following my treatment but if I focused on all the things that I read that could fill me with worry or dread or if I came across comments that possibly were unverified, this would just fill me with fear. I would more than likely dwell on those things and that would fill my mind and consume me.

I tried to guard myself from people telling me heartbreaking stories about others who had gone or were going through similar battles. It was all so real to me now and so not only would this affect me personally, but also my heart went out to each person going through similar or worse battles. On one occasion I was having my chemo infusion on the chemo ward and in the next hospital bay there were a group of women having their chemo infusions. They were talking quite loudly about their journeys and retelling stories about others and I remember trying to block out what I could hear. It wasn't that I was burying my head in the sand, but well-meaning people

can say things that aren't helpful or encouraging. I didn't want
to hear anything negative or that would make me worry. I
needed to hear stories that would fill me with hope. It wasn't
always easy, but I tried my best to be careful who I talked to or
what I picked up to read.

We all have struggles in life that we want to overcome. If
I struggled with healthy eating and I wanted to stop myself
from eating too much sugar, I would avoid the local sweet
shops. If alcohol was something I needed to avoid, I would
not drive myself to my nearest off-licence and have a browse. I
would want to put everything in place to guard myself.

'And the peace of God, which transcends all understanding,
will guard your hearts and your minds in Christ Jesus' (Phil.
4:7, NIV). When we ask God to fill our hearts with his peace,
and we put things in place ourselves, this creates a barrier and
enables our hearts (us) to function at their best.

The book of Psalms reminds us that having a secure heart
will keep out fear:

> They will have no fear of bad news;
>     their hearts are steadfast, trusting in the LORD.
> Their hearts are secure, they will have no fear;
>     in the end they will look in triumph on their foes.
>
> (Ps. 112:7–8, NIV)

As I write this, two days ago our little Shih Tzu dog, Muffin,
who was almost thirteen years old, was put to sleep. We always knew that when it was her time to go we would find it
hard, as we all doted on her. She was such a cute little thing
and it wasn't difficult to spoil her. Everyone loved Muffin! She
brought us so much joy over the years. As well as growing up

with Abi and Jack, she had travelled from house to house in all our moves with ministry. However, we were all shocked about how much it affected us when she passed away. I have cried bucketfuls these last two days and my reaction has completely taken me by surprise. I always knew we would be sad but the heartache was real. I realized that she was a huge part of our family and although she wasn't a human, the loss was still painful – we loved her so much.

Darren and I decided to go for a walk yesterday evening following a sad day and as we were strolling, I was reflecting on why this was so tough for us. Muffin was a pet but we sensed the loss so deeply. It got me thinking about our hearts again and how we are so easily hurt. When we give so much love away to someone or something, it's almost as if we give away a big chunk of our hearts. However, when that love is reciprocated that chunk is replaced and it becomes a two-way giving and receiving of love. We constantly give away pieces of our hearts – some pieces are bigger than others depending on who or what we are loving. When we suffer a loss, or that love is not reciprocated, the resulting hole is left wide open – and that's what hurts. We feel that emotion so deeply.

So many people I know have gone through divorce, break-ups and the losing of loved ones. You may be reading this and have just lost a loved one to an illness like cancer; these losses can leave you with huge holes in your heart. It changes your world and for a time you wonder how you will fit into life without them.

A friend of mine, Julia Lawton, recently wrote a book called *The End of the Beginning.*[2] In it she tells her story of how her life was turned upside down when her husband suddenly passed away. She describes the pain and grief she encountered but how God helped her in rebuilding her life. I don't think our hearts completely get over some losses but we need time to fully grieve and to allow God to heal us from the pain. So although we can't always stop the things that happen to us in life and the hurt that can cause, I really believe we can be aware of how these things can shape us going forward, and Proverbs 4:23 instructs us to guard this.

So often brick walls can go up after we have been hurt, and we stop giving and receiving love altogether. We almost want to protect ourselves from ever going through that pain again. We are designed, however, to give and receive love and it is not good for us to completely shut off from this.

When the Bible tells us to 'guard our hearts' I believe the type of guard we put there is important too. I remember those big metal fireguards that I used to see around log fires or fireplaces as a child. They were there to stop us getting burnt. A metal fireguard still allowed us to see the fire and feel the warmth but just enough protection was put in place to stop us getting burnt. The fire was still functioning for what it was put there to do. If the guard had been a brick wall we wouldn't have been able to see the beauty of a log fire or to experience the warmth.

Although erecting a brick wall around our hearts can seem the safest thing to do to prevent further damage, I don't think that is the right type of guard for us. We have to find a place where we can be guarded and be aware but not completely shut off from all the good things God has for us.

**His Hands**

God's hands shield us but there are things we need to put in place too.

Going back to that verse in Proverbs, we read:

Above all else, guard your heart,
   for everything you do flows from it.

(Prov. 4:23, NIV)

This tells us that we should guard our hearts and why, and it makes it clear that this is pretty important advice. It says, 'Above all else', so it is one of the things we need to make a priority. We need to be intentional about putting things in place to protect our hearts because what we do flows from that place.

During the time of my treatment I needed to guard my heart with what I read, listened to and watched as I didn't want anything flowing into it that could affect my actions and words going forward. I knew it would affect the hope that I had and I wanted to protect that.

Going through a heartbreak or loss of any kind is tough. Our hearts hurt but God promises that he will never leave us and his hands will comfort us.

Never will I leave you;
   never will I forsake you.

(Heb. 13:5b, NIV)

Blessed are those who mourn,
   for they will be comforted.

(Matt. 5:4, NIV)

**Take a Moment . . .**

Is your heart guarded? We can often assess the fence of our hearts by the way we respond to things.

Do we take offence quickly? Are we quick to react? Do we get angry or hurt really easily?

If so, maybe we need some time to work on our hearts. Making sure we protect what we allow into our hearts and what flows from our hearts is key to keeping us emotionally and spiritually healthy.

Maybe we need to stop in this moment and assess the condition of our fences and put some things in place again.

If your heart is troubled with many things right now, ask God to fill your heart with his peace.

If you have suffered loss or your heart is hurting – allow God time to heal that broken heart.

# 7

# Face Down

The day after my ultrasound, Darren and I travelled to Cheltenham to have my MRI scan as planned. This particular scan meant I would be face down on the table and I would have to have my arms above me while the scan took place underneath. It would take twenty to twenty-five minutes and so I wondered how I was going to stay still in such an awkward position for that amount of time. However, I thought I could turn it into an opportunity to pray and hear from God – after all, I was going to be face down, so no better position for it. I almost had an expectation that God was going to speak to me and so I went to the scan that day ready to hear!

The position I was in wasn't too uncomfortable. There was a space for my face to fit and it was much better than I had thought. Once the nurse had positioned me, I lay there ready to hear from God. I wanted him to speak to me about it all. I wanted to know what he had to say and I believed I would hear from him in those moments.

The nurses had told me that the scan would be particularly noisy and to expect lots of banging and knocking noises. They gave me headphones so I could listen to music but as the noises of the scan started I couldn't hear much – and that was OK, as I wanted to pray anyway. I wanted to hear God's voice so I asked the Holy Spirit to speak to me.

The scan started and all of a sudden there was a siren-type alarm going off and a loud banging noise – just as the nurses had said would happen. However, as I lay there praying, the noises of the scan seemed to illustrate a scenario that I could picture. I was picturing a battle that was happening above me. The knocking and banging I was hearing from the scan began to morph into the noise of the battle.

Throughout these last few weeks, I knew people had been travailing in prayer for me. Abi had become a little prayer warrior and I had a picture of Abi and me fighting in the battle in prayer with swords. I could sense the fierce battle that was above me. We were fighting the fear and dread and the cancer. When the noise of the scan got louder my praying seemed to get louder over it and the fighting got more intense – it was like waging a war. The noise of the scan and the picture of the battle I was seeing went on for some time. It was as though the battle above me represented the battle I was in and this was being fought by prayer, by the power of prayer.

Suddenly, there was a break in the scan and the noises stopped. The picture of the battle ceased . . . and there in the silence, I saw a picture of the cross – it stood bold and powerful. Behind the brown wooden cross was a background of a yellow, pink and orange sky and the cross stood out in front of the colourful backdrop. I remembered the words Jesus said on the cross that day: 'It is finished.'

The message of the cross was enough.

The cross stands as a reminder that Jesus has already won the battle. It's astonishing when we think of what he did for us and what the cross resembles. Jesus had paid the price for us and already won the victory over sin and death – and what a moment to be reminded of the power of the cross, face down in an MRI tube.

I was conscious that I had to keep very still but as it was such a powerful experience for me I was trying hard to contain the shaking inside. I came off that table changed. Something had happened to me in those moments that stayed with me throughout my treatment and will stay with me for the rest of my life. I got in the car and could barely get my words out to Darren. The realization, this reminder, of what Jesus did for me (and you!) was a turning point for me. Even before my treatment had started I felt the battle had been won and I was filled with such a peace inside knowing this was all in his hands and he was in control.

Scripture tells us what Jesus did for us all. He died for our sins. The Bible also reminds us that he *bore our diseases*: 'He himself bore our sins in his body on the tree, that we might die to sin and live to righteousness. By his wounds you have been healed' (1 Pet. 2:24, ESV).

In Matthew 8 we read an account of when Jesus healed Peter's mother-in-law. That same day he healed many that were sick and demon possessed. Matthew 8:17 (NIV) says:

> This was to fulfil what was spoken through the prophet Isaiah:
> 'He took up our infirmities
>     and bore our diseases.'

### His Hands

A few years ago, the Aspire ministry had a theme, 'Be Still'. We ran conferences based on the theme and even wore T-shirts with the words printed on them. The theme was based on a Scripture we find in the book of Psalms: 'Be still, and know that I am God . . .' (Ps. 46:10, NIV).

That was, and still is, a reminder to us all in our busy lives. We, as women, are generally good at juggling jobs, families and homes and sometimes we need that reminder to stop, to let go and to be still before God.

Going back to the story in the Bible when Moses was leading the Israelites out of Egypt to the promised land, their journey at one point led them to the Red Sea. There was no going back. They were faced with this blockage, a huge hurdle, a 'mountain' that was the sea. The people panicked and they blamed Moses. They began to question him, saying they would have been better off as slaves in Egypt. You can almost picture the chaos, the fear, the realization of what they were faced with. I'm sure Moses began to sweat a little as the pressure was on him. However, Moses faced the people in the midst of the panic and uncertainty and we read in Exodus his response: 'The LORD will fight for you; you need only to be still' (Exod. 14:14, NIV). Here was a time when they just needed to be still and trust God.

God had clearly spoken to me while I was being still on the MRI table. It took a situation where I had no other choice than to be still to show me the most important thing I needed to know in this journey I was on: a reminder of who God is and what he had done for me. No greater love.

Sometimes in our busyness and in our times of stress and worry we simply need to listen to him. We need to give him opportunities to speak. However, being still doesn't always mean standing still and not going anywhere. We read in the following verses in Exodus that the Lord prompted Moses to tell the Israelites to move on. The Israelites didn't need to stand still and wait – they needed to keep moving. However, being still in this moment meant they had to be still in their hearts and trust that God would fight for them. They had to keep moving forward in their journey but with an assurance about who God was.

Sometimes, when we are faced with a situation – a diagnosis, perhaps – it's easy to spiral into a blind panic. In these moments it's important that we still our hearts and remember he is God and he fights for us. This can bring the focus off the problem and back to him. God's hands parted the Red Sea – he had a plan. His hands not only protect, lead and comfort us but they are hands that fight our battles and part our 'seas' too.

## Take a Moment . . .

What situations are you trying to fix? Are they consuming you right now and robbing you of your peace?

Ask God to show you what you need to let go of – and as you do, be still and confident knowing he is able to fight our battles for us.

If you are reading this and you are in a health battle, just be reminded of the power of the cross.

Jesus died for us and what he did for us that day is something we must never forget when we go through storms.

There is no greater love than this, so take a moment to be still and allow the truth of what he did for you that day fill you with a peace and a comfort.

As you go forward, allow your heart to be still in the knowledge that he has you in the palm of his hand.

# 8

# Rope Holders

Throughout my treatment, family and friends came alongside me to pray and support me. I chose not to go on social media and talk about my diagnosis as in those early days I didn't want people feeling sorry for me. Social media can be a great place to connect and encourage people but it can sometimes also be used in a negative way too and, as I said in Chapter 6, I needed to guard my heart as much as I could so this was a decision I made early on.

In the Bible we read a story of Peter walking on water with Jesus – when he took his eyes off Jesus, he began to sink. I wanted to keep my eyes on Jesus throughout this journey – I didn't want to sink by coming across things that would instil fear. I always said the only time I would talk about it on social media was after my treatment – to give God praise!

My treatment was happening during the Covid-19 lock-down so not seeing other people very much was normal during this time. People were not going out and about so, unless you knew about my situation, not seeing me around at work or other places was not abnormal. I also found it hard telling people about my diagnosis. That I was going through a cancer battle was something I never thought I would hear myself say, and the reality of what I was going through would hit me each time I'd say it, so apart from those close to me I allowed the news to just get out there naturally. That did mean, however, that some friends only found out at the end of my treatment and so for that – I do apologize! But I just tried to navigate the situation in the best way I knew how.

I think it's OK for you to travel such journeys however you feel best and you should at no time feel pressure from anyone to have to behave in a certain way. We all deal with things differently and the added pressure of making sure you are pleasing everyone in the process is something you do not need. Those who love and care for you will understand.

I could not write a book about my journey and not mention about the support I did receive. However, I wanted to write about this not just to mention how grateful I am, but also to highlight how much love and support means to someone going through something like this. I didn't want to completely block everyone out of my life during that time, like erecting a brick wall around myself. Although I needed to protect myself, I needed support too – I just needed that right type of guard again.

I had many Scriptures given to me that I held on to especially during those dark times; Scriptures that were given to me in a text or message that arrived exactly at a time when I needed a reminder that God was with me and was in control; Scriptures that I held on to right through the course of my treatment that have become part of my story today. Powerful reminders when I needed them the most.

If you know or are supporting someone through a health battle, never underestimate the effect that a message, a Bible verse, or words of comfort have on that person. How often have we thought of someone who is struggling at one particular moment, but never told them? You never know how much that encouragement might have meant to them. In that moment they could have been feeling fearful or anxious, they could have received a bad report or been feeling overwhelmed by the elements of the storm they were in. Those few lines of letting them know how loved, how amazing they are – messages to cheer them on – could have arrived just when they needed them the most. You could have been God's 'postman' that day, delivering words that he wanted to say to that person.

When people started messaging me to say that they were praying for me, I really appreciated the time they spent in their day thinking of me and I valued every single prayer lifted to heaven on my behalf. I received messages, cards, flowers and gifts throughout my treatment and often these would arrive just at the right moment. Some people prayed daily for me and committed to doing so until the end of my treatment. I appreciated the love and care from all of them so much and I will be forever grateful.

When someone is going through a cancer battle or any health battle, receiving love and support from family and friends and even the local church is something that not only helps emotionally but practically too. The times my mum cooked meals, the times my dad did odd jobs, the times my husband did the ironing or my kids helped around the house all meant that I could rest and give my body time to recover from the effects of the treatment. I really believe their care and taking pressure off me with cooking and housework helped me cope as well as I did with the treatment.

I know many great churches put things in place to help those who are housebound or not well. If you belong to a local church and you are looking for ways to help those who are housebound or going through treatment but don't have the support of many family and friends, then practical support is one way that can make a huge difference. A rota for providing meals, doing food shopping, or giving car lifts for hospital appointments are all practical ways that will help an individual. They may not ask for help so reaching out to them and asking what they need will be so appreciated.

Cooking someone their favourite meal, baking them their favourite cake or taking a pile of their ironing not only allows them to rest but it's also a real treat for them! Due to the side effects of the chemo and steroids, I often craved certain foods. There was a time when I really longed for foods like jelly and blancmange or certain sweets as they soothed my throat. Asking someone going through chemo what foods they are craving at that particular time is something that is extremely helpful.

It wasn't easy for any of my family during this time. Seeing a daughter, wife, mother, sister, daughter-in-law, cousin and niece go through this is painful for any family. Members of my family were rocks to me in different ways and were truly incredible, but it is important to know that although the person who is going through a health battle needs love and support, their loved ones need it too. It was hard for them watching me undergo such brutal treatment, and I know that while they were being strong for me they too needed support.

My parents had each other to talk to and my children had the support of my husband, grandparents and their partners, but I do feel Darren didn't reach out for support as much as he should have done. He had questions and concerns and probably didn't voice them enough as he was trying to be strong for me and everyone else. It was only when I saw him break down when I received good results from one particular scan that I realized how much he was carrying. He stayed positive throughout my treatment and he helped me practically as well as spiritually. He gave me space to travel this in the way I thought best even when I know he didn't know what to say or do to make it better. I do feel looking back that he needed someone who he could be really honest with. I know one or two friends did reach out to him and he often talks about how much this meant to him. I'm so grateful to them.

I think often it's harder for men to admit they need support as they maybe feel it's their role to be the strong, tough one. If you are a husband, son or father reading this who is caring for a loved one and feeling you need someone to talk to, please do reach out for help. It's OK to tell a friend, doctor, pastor or family member that you are struggling or that you have questions. It is never a weakness to ask for help.

Jack, my son, would admit that the way he dealt with my diagnosis and treatment was to withdraw a little. He struggled to see me go through it. I thought it would be good for Jack to express some of his feelings.

### *Jack's thoughts . . .*

I remember having dreams when I was younger about either my mum or dad having cancer. I guess it was a deep-down fear of mine as a child. The thought of my parents going through this and the possibility of losing one of them was obviously something that used to play on my mind a lot.

Initially when my mum told me she had breast cancer I remember being in shock, and I had all these questions and thoughts running through my mind about what this meant and what would happen to her. I didn't really know enough about breast cancer and I guess hearing those words was bringing true something I had never wanted to hear.

My mum went through her treatment during Covid so it meant I spent a lot of time in my bedroom or watching TV. I couldn't really keep myself busy as we couldn't go anywhere due to the lockdowns. I found this hard and looking back I think I dealt with it by sleeping lots and even comfort eating. I guess my way of dealing with it was to shut myself off from it. However, I had a deep-down confidence that my mum would get through this and she would be ok. I think God gave me a peace inside.

When my mum started her chemo treatment, each day I could see the effect it was having on her physically. This was difficult for me to see and if I'm honest, at times I found it hard to even look at her. This was because seeing her hair fall out was a reminder to me of what she was battling. There were times when she looked tired and weak but I kept reminding myself this was because of the treatment.

Christmas was different that year and I don't think any of us really felt like celebrating. My birthday was in the January too and I remember my mum got taken into hospital just before it as she was fighting an infection. That day was hard for my mum as she just wanted to be with me. I remember I didn't really want to open my birthday cards as it just wasn't the same without her there.

Looking back I probably should have talked about my concerns more rather than keeping them in. If anyone is reading this and you are watching your mum or someone you love go through a health battle, reach out to someone. No questions are too silly. Bottling up your emotions isn't good for you and talking about it really does help.

Jack

It is important to look out for those men and women who are caring for family members. Just a quick phone call or text message to ask how *they* are and whether they would like a break – a coffee, perhaps – could give them an opportunity to open up and feel supported too.

Apart from my family, who I will thank personally at the end of the book, there were certain individuals who felt prompted to pray for me throughout my treatment. They prayed with faith on my behalf that God would bring me through it. I had friends who would meet on Zoom weekly to pray with and for me, even though at times I couldn't join them as I felt too tired or weak.

When you are going through a health battle, having the support of family and close friends is immeasurable, but also knowing that others are putting aside time to pray for you really fills and surrounds you with comfort too. I don't want to mention names as I would run the risk of leaving someone out unintentionally, but you all know who you are and I value the love you showed during my time of need. However, I wanted to mention one or two of those people purely because their support was unexpected.

What surprised me during this time was the love and care I received from those that I had not seen for years. Old work colleagues, friends whom I had lost contact with, and wider family members suddenly got in touch and stayed in contact throughout my journey. Just because we lose touch with people doesn't mean they don't care about what happens to us. After years of not seeing each other the kindness of these people showed me that even though life can take us in different directions, true friendship remains.

There were some on this journey who God prompted to stand shoulder to shoulder with me even though they lived far away from me at the time. There were others who felt urged to pray for me who hadn't even met me.

Anne Eskelin was a best pal of my mum growing up. She had moved to America many years ago. When she heard of my diagnosis she decided to gather a group of her friends to pray for me throughout my treatment. They called themselves my 'US rope holders'.

In Luke 5 and Mark 2 in the Bible, we read a story about a group of men who brought a paralysed man to Jesus. They couldn't find a way in to the house where Jesus was due to the crowds, so they decided to go on the roof and lower the man down to Jesus on a mat. They did what they could to bring him before Jesus, who saw their faith and made the man well.

This story is an example of how we too can bring those that need healing before the feet of Jesus. I think about the effort and faith this group of men showed that day. Practically it must have been very difficult getting the paralysed man not only through the crowds, but on to the roof top of a house. Even when they had managed to get to that point, they then had to dig an opening in the roof and find a way to lower him down to Jesus on a mat. What faith did these men show!

I am thankful to God for many friends and family that became my rope holders throughout my breast cancer journey, those who sacrificed time out of their day to take me to Jesus' feet in prayer.

Apart from Anne, I didn't know the other women, but they chose to lift me up in prayer constantly. I received cards from Anne almost weekly and often received cards from the other ladies whom I had never met. These cards and gifts would arrive from the USA just as I needed encouragement to keep going. They took time to write to me, and their kindness and faith is something I will never forget.

There are always things we can do to help others if we look out for them, and your love and care will impact an individual in more ways than you can imagine. If you have heard of someone you once knew going through a health battle and you don't know whether it's been too long to get back in touch – just do it! It will mean so much to them.

My cousin, Rachel, who doesn't live near us, and her daughter Abi (who was travelling through Mexico at the time) called themselves my 'Aaron and Hur'. In Exodus 17 we read that when the Israelites were in battle with the Amalekites, as long as Moses' hands were up in the air the Israelites were winning the battle. So, when Moses became tired, Aaron and Hur held up Moses' arms.

This mother and daughter wanted to be my Aaron and Hur – to lift up my arms in prayer when I got tired. I have a large wider family that are spread out all over the UK and although we don't get to see each other much, we are always there for each other. Even though Abi was travelling on the other side of the world, with time differences, she never failed to remember hospital appointments and treatment dates and prayed constantly, as did her mum.

I didn't see Abi and Rachel or any of my 'US rope holders' during my treatment but their constant connection to me during this time taught me how important it is to be obedient when you feel you should pray for someone. Being on the receiving end, and knowing how comforting it was that they were doing this for me, taught me so much about taking the time to love others as Jesus taught.

I will never forget the love and kindness that people showed me. The thought of people stopping in their day to think and pray for me touched my heart and it taught me so much about the importance of family and friendship.

It is also important to note that when you go through an illness like this, sometimes people can react differently from what you expect. Some find it hard and don't know what to say. They might distance themselves from you. Often we can be surprised with friends who we thought would be a tower of strength to us, but aren't what we thought they would be. It's easy to take offence or think they don't care. In reality, those people might not know how to react, and might think you need the space, so they distance themselves. Some people find these situations really difficult and don't cope very well with them. Some feel they don't know what to say. It doesn't always mean they don't care. Looking back, I do wonder if I gauged things right and showed my support enough to others during times when they needed it.

I understand not everyone reading this may have a strong network of support or a family during such times. Knowing how this helped me through my journey with cancer has made me realize the importance of keeping an eye out for those that don't have support of a family.

There are many great organizations and charities out there that offer great support and advice. I have listed some at the back of this book for reference. They do make such a difference in the lives of so many people, and the work they do is incredible. However, even if you haven't a natural family around you, having a circle of support from friends is important in helping you feel loved and not alone.

If you are reading this and your friend is going through a health battle, maybe they haven't got a family around them for whatever reason. Maybe gathering a couple of their friends and providing a really tight network of support for them during this time will make all the difference to them. A text message, an email, a cake, a meal, a card means more than you

ever know. The timing of these for me was, as I said, often
when I needed it the most.

If you yourself have a current health problem, just know
that however big or small your circle of support is, it's OK
to reach out and ask for more help if you need it. People will
want to know whether to come close or whether they should
give you space, and are often just waiting for the cues. There
will be people in your neighbourhood who want to help so
even if you don't have many family or friends around, please
do let someone know this is the case for you – even if it's your
local church or hospital.

It's equally OK if you want to travel your journey more
privately and to keep a tighter circle of support. There were
times during my treatment when I didn't want to explain how
I was feeling that particular day, because I was tired and going
through the events of the day was almost too much. It's OK if
you don't want to see people or spend time replying to lots of
well-meaning messages. People will understand if you let them
know – just be honest. Asking a family member or friend to
get messages around for you can also be really helpful.

## His Hands

Whatever your circle of support looks like, you can know that
your biggest help comes from the Lord and we read this in the
book of Psalms:

> I lift up my eyes to the mountains –
>     where does my help come from?

My help comes from the Lord,
    the Maker of heaven and earth.

He will not let your foot slip –
    he who watches over you will not slumber;
indeed, he who watches over Israel
    will neither slumber nor sleep.

The Lord watches over you –
    the Lord is your shade at your right hand;
the sun will not harm you by day,
    nor the moon by night.

The Lord will keep you from all harm –
    he will watch over your life;
the Lord will watch over your coming and going
    both now and for evermore.

(Ps. 121:1–8, NIV)

What an assurance it is to know that the Lord is watching over you. Not everyone gets it right in the area of support, but there is constant help, love and strength from above that is the biggest comfort and strength. There were times when I felt the loving arms around me. There were times when I felt scared but I knew God had a grip on me. There were times when his hands were a shield, keeping me from all harm and even when I slept he was watching over me. The Lord knows you better than anyone, so be real to him.

When I think of the love I was shown and how my family have demonstrated a love that is sacrificial, isn't this how Jesus wants us to love? We read in Scripture about how important this is to Jesus: 'My command is this: love each other as I have loved you. Greater love has no-one than this: to lay down one's life for one's friends' (John 15:12–13, NIV).

This was not just important to Jesus, but a commandment! However, he didn't just *command* this, he *demonstrated* it. While Jesus was on this earth he was our biggest example of how we should love and serve others; he came to serve. His hands served, healed the sick, performed miracles and comforted those who needed it but, even more than this, his hands bore the nail prints of the greatest love ever to be shown to me and you. No greater love. 'For even the Son of Man did not come to be served, but to serve, and to give his life as a ransom for many' (Mark 10:45, NIV).

**Take a Moment . . .**

Look at your circle of support right now. Does that circle need to enlarge – do you need more support, help and friendship?

If you feel alone or isolated, please know that there are people who care out there so please do reach out.

If you don't attend a church, why not look at going along one week? You could contact some local churches in your area if you are housebound. You might make some new friends and soon feel as though you have a brand new family! You will also get to know about a loving heavenly Father who will always be there for you to lean on. You are never alone.

Your local GP and hospitals can also provide you with details of organizations that can help you. Alternatively, the Samaritans are a great organization to contact if you just need someone to talk to.

We should also be on the lookout for those who need someone to talk to, who need a listening ear. They won't always ask you for help.

Jesus told the parable of the good Samaritan in Luke 10: a story of the most unexpected person showing love to someone in need. Jesus told us that we needed to do likewise.

We need to be alert and seek out not only those in our close network of friends and family who need support, but those in our communities too.

Maybe ask God today to show you or bring someone into your path who needs your love and care.

# 9

# Infused

My first chemo was given on 11 January, and I was a bit appre-
hensive beforehand, not knowing what to expect or how I was
going to react to it. I was going to attempt the 'cold cap' so my
mum had cut my hair shorter for me to make it easier to wear.
The cold cap is a helmet-type hat and they fill the lining with
water and freeze it. You need to wear the cap while chemo is
being administered. The findings were that some women kept
their hair during chemo treatment or their hair just thinned
rather than fall out completely. There was a 50/50 chance of
it working and, being the determined person I am, I just had
to give this a go. Many women don't attempt it as I guess it
is a bit gruelling and that on top of having chemo itself can
be too much to cope with. However, I was told that the first
ten minutes were the worst and if I could keep it on for that
amount of time initially, it would get easier.

One type of chemo I was given for my first three cycles was
bright red in colour – probably a fitting colour for what it did.
For each of these cycles I would watch this red 'poison' being
put through my veins. As it went in, I always thought about
what it was about to do to my cells and it was something I
didn't want pumped through my body for so many reasons.
However, on the other hand, I desperately wanted it to de-
stroy the cancer that had invaded my body so I knew it was
going to be vital too.

Before my chemo started, I had received a Scripture from
one of my friends which was a great encouragement: 'Now my
beloved ones, I have saved these most important truths for last:
Be supernaturally infused with strength through your life-un-
ion with the Lord Jesus. Stand victorious with the force of his
explosive power flowing in and through you' (Eph. 6:10, TPT).
I would declare the words in this Scripture while I watched

the chemicals going into my veins. Even though this treatment looked brutal, and was brutal, I trusted that something supernatural was also being pumped through my veins during the infusion and that, as the verse says, I would 'stand victorious'. I prayed with every cycle of chemo that through this treatment God would protect me from the effects and heal me through it.

The side effects of chemo can be unpleasant and, although as time went on I experienced a few, I was grateful that I could cope OK with the ones I was having. This was another answer to prayer on my gift tag at Christmas! I thank God I coped with it and although there were times when it was hard, I was very grateful I got through each treatment. I know people react differently to chemo but it always amazed me what drugs were available to help with any side effect patients experienced. The doctors tweaked and adjusted the dosage to suit me and I was given medication that offered some sort of relief from most things. I was so thankful for the care and treatment I had from the NHS and it made me realize how blessed we are to have such incredible doctors and scientists.

As each chemo session passed, I got to know how I was roughly going to feel during certain days in the cycles. Although the rock-bottom days where my white blood cells had dropped right down were hard, I knew that I would soon feel better as they started to come back up. Knowing how it worked and why I felt so bad helped me cope with it.

However, on around day seven or eight in the first cycle I started to have a really sore throat – a feeling I knew all too well when starting to have tonsillitis. I did think that perhaps it was a reaction to the white blood cells depleting so I wondered if it was all part of the reaction to the drugs. However, as time went on I felt really poorly.

It is important to check your temperature during the low cell-count days to make sure you haven't contracted an infection. To pick up an infection when you have nothing to fight it with is not ideal. This is something that can happen often so I was being super-careful with everything I touched or ate. However, along with feeling really unwell, my temperature started to go up and so I was admitted to Cheltenham Hospital. They checked my blood and discovered I was neutropenic, which meant I had a very low quantity of white blood cells. This is normal in the chemo cycle but it means that it is harder for the body to fight any infection. My count that day wasn't just low but on zero! My bloods were showing that I had an infection in my body and so I needed to be pumped with antibiotics quickly. Although I was pretty sure it was tonsillitis they labelled the condition as 'neutropenic sepsis'. I couldn't believe this was happening during my very first chemo cycle.

I was in hospital for a few days until the antibiotics and the treatment given to boost the production of my white blood cells was beginning to work. Even though I was alone in hospital, uncertain as to what was going to happen, I didn't feel lonely. Again, I knew God was holding my hand. Although I felt very weak, I was so grateful I got through that storm and I knew that during this journey I needed to trust God and hold on through every step. Even though the nurses and doctors were wonderful there, I prayed that I would never need to return there again and I thank God I didn't.

I had an appointment with my oncologist a week or so later, just before cycle number two, to see how I was coping. When I had been admitted to hospital with the infection, they had routinely taken a chest X-ray. As nothing was mentioned, I didn't think any more about it. However, during our meeting, the oncologist told me that on the X-ray another area had been flagged up. As he said those words, my heart sank and I began to tremble. He didn't think the area, which was by my lower ribs, was anything nasty but he didn't know what it was. He told me that he needed to be reassured, so I needed a CT scan.

I left the appointment shattered again at the thought of having to deal with something else. It felt that no sooner I had got over one hurdle than there was another one in front of me. I could feel fear starting to grip me again but I needed to hold on to the Scriptures and trust that God was in control.

**His Hands**

There are times in life when we need to reach out and hold God's hands. Yes, those hands are there to hold us in times of need but there are times where I felt I needed to reach out myself and hold on to him too.

In Mark 5 we read about the story of Jairus, a ruler's daughter. She was dying and, in another account of this story in Luke 8, it even says they thought she was dead. Jesus started making his way to Jairus' house and we read that crowds of people were gathering around him. Within this story, another story emerges. Among the crowds, a woman with a great need and great faith reached out to Jesus. She felt if only she could touch the hem of his garment she would be healed.

There were a few things that struck me in this story. We learn that both women were important to Jesus – important enough to want to know who had reached out to him and important enough to wade through the crowds and go to the girl who was dying. A young girl aged twelve and a woman who had been suffering for twelve years . . . both situations looked impossible. Everyone thought the girl was dead and the woman who had reached out had been to lots of physicians. Both seemed impossible situations but a 'reaching out' changed everything. As the woman reached out she was healed and as Jesus reached out to the girl, she was healed.

There are times in our lives when Jesus reaches out to us with his hands and there are times when we, like the woman, need to reach out to him. You can read the story in Luke 8:43–8. There is so much we can take from this passage but one point is how the woman had had this issue for twelve years . . . but she did not give up! Her condition made her unclean in the eyes of people so she could have easily hidden away, ashamed to even be out and about, but something that day made her rise up – she wasn't going to take this anymore. She fought through the crowds and reached out to Jesus. Her reach made a difference, her reach changed everything for her that day. When Jesus stopped and realized what had happened, what struck him wasn't her action, but her faith.

So often, we can wait for circumstances to change and, yes, there are times that Jesus comes into the midst of our situation and takes us by the hand, but sometimes we need the faith to reach out to him too.

When I was in the hospital having received my first chemo and fighting an infection, and when I was in the oncologist's room being told this new information, I immediately felt the need to reach out and grab the hand of Jesus. In both those moments I was alone and things seemed uncertain, but I knew I needed his strength to face the setbacks and he was right there ready to take hold of my hand with his.

**Take a Moment . . .**

In the previous chapter I talked about the importance of reaching out to others.

Sometimes when you are in the 'eye of the storm' you need to know that Jesus is with you in your boat. Reaching out and holding on to him is maybe all you can do today.

Just know he sees what you are going through and is there with you.

There were times in my journey when I felt that Jesus was already there, waiting for me to reach out to him, and knowing that he was there with me in those moments gave me great peace. He had gone before me in the operating theatre, in the doctor's room, in the chemo unit. There was great comfort knowing he was sitting right beside me.

Whatever you are going through today, whatever you are facing today, reach out and lean on him.

Tell him your worries, tell him what you may be scared about, and ask him to fill you with a peace that only he can give.

# 10

# Tent Times

During my treatment, I was grateful that the house was busy during the day. I valued the company and support of my family but sometimes, even though I was trying to be strong, I would go to bed at night and just cry. In those moments I was probably processing what was happening to me. Due to Covid-19 being around, we decided Darren would sleep in our other spare room during my chemo treatment, to guard me further from any seasonal bugs that he might pick up and pass to me. So our bedroom at that part of my day became my 'tent time' with God.

Going back to the story of Moses, in Exodus, we read the importance of the 'tent times' he had with God:

> Now Moses used to take a tent and pitch it outside the camp some distance away, calling it the 'tent of meeting.' Anyone enquiring of the LORD would go to the tent of meeting outside the camp. And whenever Moses went out to the tent, all the people rose and stood at the entrances to their tents, watching Moses until he entered the tent. As Moses went into the tent, the pillar of cloud would come down and stay at the entrance, while the LORD spoke with Moses. Whenever the people saw the pillar of cloud standing at the entrance to the tent, they all stood and worshipped, each at the entrance to their tent. The LORD would speak to Moses face to face, as one speaks to a friend. Then Moses would return to the camp, but his young assistant Joshua son of Nun did not leave the tent.

(Exod. 33: 7–11, NIV)

This tent of meeting was a place of solitude for Moses. It was far away from everyone else in the camp. It was a place where Moses was still before the Lord and it was here that he received instruction and wisdom. This was a place where the presence of God was, and it was where God spoke to Moses 'as one speaks with a friend'. This tent was a special place where Moses came away from the busyness of life to hear God and spend time with him. I love the part where it says, 'but his young assistant Joshua son of Nun did not leave the tent.' This makes me smile as I'm sure that after the presence of God filled that tent he would most certainly not want to leave!

I preached about this passage of Scripture a few years ago and I encouraged women to get their special place with God, a place where it could just be 'you and him'. I talked about how important this was and how God longs to speak to us in this place. I talked about how this was a place where we could be real with him. Little did I know that the tent of meeting in my own personal life during this season was going to be as special as it was.

My 'tent' became a place where I sometimes cried, where I worshipped and where I was still before God. This was a place where I was real before him – a place to pour my heart out to him. Worship was powerful during this time. With all that happened throughout the day, whether that was hospital appointments, chemo treatment or just navigating the effects of the chemo, coming to my tent at the end of the day helped me to stay focused on Jesus. Every time I could feel my mind starting to fill with the uncertainty of the outcome, I knew I needed to get to my tent and worship. I always felt uplifted and at peace afterwards. Usually everyone was in bed when I had my tent times and so I would put my ear phones in and 'silently' sing out. I would be sat in bed, with my arms stretched out, and I would be singing from my heart and I worshipped with every fibre of my being.

There were a few worship songs that became special to me during this time but one in particular was 'Your Name' by Life Church Worship.[3] The words of this song focus on the power of the name of Jesus and the more I sang this song, the more I realized that there was nothing greater than his name. I had sung about the name of Jesus many times but the truth of these words became a reality to me in these moments. Each time I sang it, I could sense the presence of God. I would place my hand over the cancer lump and speak the name of Jesus over it. I just repeated his name over and over. There really was nothing stronger, nothing greater and nothing higher. Healing and freedom are in his name and I knew I was singing this truth over the disease. Because my chemo was reduced in dosage, I often wondered if it was working, but in these times spent worshipping I knew Jesus' name was even more powerful than chemo. It was almost as though this song was written about this season of my life – even from when we had that moment in the car with the mountains. The chorus goes like this:

There is power, power, power in the name
Healing, freedom, peace I can't explain
Mountains bow, walls come down at the name of Jesus
There is nothing greater, there is nothing greater than
    your name.

I realized that what God was showing us that day in the car, when we were drawn to the mountains, now all made sense. I remembered Abi saying to me that day that what we were seeing meant something but she didn't know what the significance was. The video I took of the mountain disappearing was what I now believed he would do with the cancer. The amazing thing was that when I realized this, I scrambled through the videos on my phone to find that clip. As I played it, the song that was playing in the car at that moment was this very song: 'Your Name' by Life Worship. I didn't know the song then but Darren did, and had put it on.

Another part of the song says:

There's only one; His name is Jesus
Death won't have the final say, it's finished
When the stone was rolled away
There's only one; His name is Jesus.

This song became so special to me. As I sang these words, I was taken back to the moment in the MRI room when I saw the picture of the cross and I was reminded of the words that Jesus said: 'It is finished.' I believed with all my heart that, as I sang these words and held my hand over the lump, the name of Jesus was all-powerful over the cancer and it had no choice other than to go.

Going for the CT scan on the area by my ribs was difficult. I was having the second round of chemo and the appointment date was during the low days of the chemo cycle. I had a good enough excuse not to go that day and maybe to rearrange the appointment but, as I sat on the edge of the bed, tired and weak, I knew I needed to face this. I needed to reach and take hold of his hand again.

As the CT scanner went over me I just declared the name of Jesus over my body and said his name over and over again. What I believed and received in those tent times as I worshipped and sang out to him, I needed to take with me into the world, and as I lay there I believed there was nothing greater than his name!


## His Hands

In the journey that I found myself on, I was not only learning daily about his hands but also about the power of the name of Jesus. In my tent times, as I called on his name and prayed over the cancer, I really believed, as the Scriptures said, that he would heal me.

> You may ask me for anything in my name, and I will do it.
> (John 14:14, NIV)

> And whatever you do, whether in word or deed, do it all in the name of the Lord Jesus, giving thanks to God the Father through him.
> (Col. 3:17, NIV)

> I have given you authority to trample on snakes and scorpions and to overcome all the power of the enemy; nothing will harm you.
> (Luke 10:19, NIV)

I love the story of Esther. She was at a place in her life where it would seem to many that she had everything. She had beauty, the king chose her, the king was in love with her and even before she was presented to the king, she had twelve months of beauty treatments. I am sure every woman right now will understand how blessed she was! She must have been the envy of most of the women around her but we go on to read that Esther was presented with a situation – a request from her cousin that meant she needed to come before the king and risk her life to try to save the Jews.

I am sure Esther paused; risking this whole life of royalty and favour was something of a big ask. She had been presented with a request that could potentially change everything for a whole bunch of people but it would also mean she would possibly lose so much herself. So what did she do? 'Then Esther sent this reply to Mordecai: "Go, gather together all the Jews who are in Susa, and fast for me. Do not eat or drink for three days, night or day. I and my attendants will fast as you do. When this is done, I will go to the king, even though it is against the law. And if I perish, I perish"' (Esth. 4:15–16, NIV).

It doesn't say in the Bible that Esther ran to everyone else for advice. She knew what she needed to do to get advice, and I'm sure she went to her 'tent'. She knew she had to come before God to pray and fast, to be still before him and to hear God in this situation.

We read in chapter five what Esther did next: 'On the third day Esther put on her royal robes and stood in the inner court of the palace, in front of the king's hall. The king was sitting on his royal throne in the hall, facing the entrance' (Esth. 5:1, NIV).

So after fasting for three days, Esther put on her royal robes and stood. What a picture! She stood in the confidence of who her God was and what she felt him telling her to do. She had had her 'tent time' in prayer and fasting and I believe in that place she had overcame the panic, the what ifs, the worry, the decision of what to do. Her confidence was in the God she trusted, so she could stand in that authority.

Sometimes, we need to come before God and be still. When we give God time to speak to us, to give us wisdom and instruction, we can then face our problem with a confidence and strength that comes from him. God's hands hold ours so when we need to stand and face something we can stand there with our royal robes on (knowing who we are in him) and face it head on.

**Take a Moment . . .**

Why not find your 'tent' – whether that's a room in your house, a place in your garden or even in your car on your way to work – and make it a place where you regularly come and spend time with God?

Make it a place where you offload, where you are real before him.

Tell him if you feel scared or frightened.

Make your 'tent' a place where you listen to instruction, where you worship him, where you face your fears.

When we focus on how great he is, our eyes are off our problems and on to the one who can solve them. Those places can become a powerhouse!

He is already waiting for you in your tent.

# 11

# Grateful

A week or so later, while I was waiting for the results of the CT scan, I received a letter in the post. It was a letter from the hospital asking me to go for a bone scan. As I sat there for a few moments, with the letter in my hand, I wondered what this could mean. Was this a routine appointment for someone going through breast cancer? Or had the CT scan showed something else that they needed to investigate? I quickly rang my oncologist as I didn't know whether this was something I should be concerned about, but he was on holiday so I spoke to a breast nurse.

After looking into it, the nurse explained that they had the results of the CT scan – which showed that the area of concern near my ribs was nothing more than what they called 'fat pads'. I had never heard of fat pads before but whatever they were I was relieved to have them. I was so thankful that this wasn't anything serious. However, the nurse told me that the CT scan showed I had some marks or lesions on my bones that they needed a closer look at. So, just when I was receiving good news, again I was faced with other suspicious-looking areas in my body. The nurse asked whether I had had previous sports injuries that could have caused injuries to my bones, but I was never really a sporty person and so I couldn't think of any times that I had injured myself. The bone scan would show what these areas were so I just needed to wait for my appointment.

Waiting for this in-depth bone scan was probably one of the most testing times for us all, as nobody really knew what this news meant. I couldn't give a reason for these lesions so I found myself assuming they must be something serious. I could feel a panic starting to set in so I went to the Scriptures – Scriptures that I could hold on to, Scriptures that I could pray over my body. I was learning that each time fear started to fill me, I had to pitch my tent in the land of hope and fix my eyes on Jesus. The following Scriptures I found regarding bones become a source of strength to me during the waiting period.

And the LORD will guide you continually
    and satisfy your desire in scorched places
    and make your bones strong;
and you shall be like a watered garden,
    like a spring of water,
    whose waters do not fail.

(Isa. 58:11, ESV)

Be gracious to me, O LORD, for I am languishing;
    heal me, O LORD, for my bones are troubled.

(Ps. 6:2, ESV)

He keeps all his bones;
    not one of them is broken.

(Ps. 34:20, ESV)

I prayed these Scriptures over my body asking the Lord to make 'my bones strong', that he would 'be gracious to me and heal me' and that not one bone would be 'troubled' or 'broken'. I asked again if he would change the picture. I believed he had done it previously and I believed whatever this showed, he could do it again.

I had my halfway appointment with the breast surgeon the day before my bone scan. This was an ultrasound scan to see how the chemo was working. The surgeon was pleased as the lump had reduced to about 1.2cms so he was pretty confident that by the end of the chemo the tumour would have completely or almost gone. I was so thankful the treatment was working and came away giving praise to Jesus.

The following day I went to the hospital for the bone scan and again as the noisy machine scanned over my body I prayed, declaring the name of Jesus. During my appointment Abi was at home praying, storming the heavens again on my behalf. As I had left for the hospital that day, she had known how concerned I was and it had troubled her, but I could see as I walked back through the doors from the hospital that she looked different, as though the weight of the worry had lifted. She had been interceding in prayer for me and really believed God had already answered our prayers. She had gone to her 'tent' and prayed, declaring healing over my body. I was so aware that this journey I was on wasn't just growing my faith but also the faith of my children.

The results of that scan showed nothing amiss. I truly believe God heard our prayers and changed the picture. I couldn't wait to get back into my tent that day to thank and praise him (silently!).

The last three chemo treatments were a different type, and somewhat stronger; again the dosage needed to be tweaked as the side effects I was having were proving it was too strong. I was so relieved to receive the sixth, final one. As anyone knows going through this treatment, each cycle is like a blow to your body and you do get tired and weary. Even though I hated the poison going through my veins, I thanked God for chemo. After the last infusion it was time for me to ring the bell on the ward as I left.

This was something that the nurses encouraged those who had finished treatment to do as a sign that they had completed it. It really was a sound that came as a relief and as I rang it there that day, I rang it as a celebration that the six rounds of treatment were completed; it was a ring of thanks. I was grateful to the doctors and nurses and for the hospital itself, and to my God for bringing me through it. That bell rang with a heart of real gratitude that this part of my treatment was completed.

The scan following my last treatment showed there was a very tiny amount of the cancer left, and the breast surgeon at the time wasn't even sure whether this was just scar tissue, it was so small. I would know more after I had had my operation and further tests would have been done, but he was happy with the outcome and again I gave God all the glory and praise.

As my blood tests had shown that I carried the altered BRCA 1 gene, it was advised that I would need a double mastectomy and the removal of both of my ovaries and tubes. The faulty gene meant that there was not only a risk of breast cancer but ovarian cancer too, so these operations were preventative measures and reduced the risk of the cancer returning. The double mastectomy was scheduled a few weeks after my last chemo and then my ovaries would be taken out a couple of months later.

Having a double mastectomy was something I was preparing myself for throughout my chemo treatment. It wasn't a difficult decision when it was suggested to me as I knew it needed to happen. In some ways it gave me some sort of relief; without it but knowing that I had this faulty gene, I would be forever more checking my breasts and experiencing the fear that process would bring each time.

Whether I would have reconstructions at the same time was something I needed to consider. If I had reconstructions, the operation would take much longer and with it would come the risk of needing further operations to rectify or tweak it. The mastectomies themselves would be a long operation so the thought of being on an operating table for a couple of hours more for a reconstruction was a concern for me. If I was having a single mastectomy maybe a reconstruction would have been an easier decision. At that time, the thought of going through the two preventative operations that were needed and then possibly further operations to correct anything from a reconstruction was a little too much for me to take in. I had just been through six rounds of chemo and my body was already tired. I wanted to be at my daughter's wedding and I didn't want to run the risk of being in hospital having corrective surgery just before that important event. I decided against reconstructive surgery.

Although I was asked to consider my decision very carefully, I didn't really struggle with it. I felt it was the right one for me, for now. I understood that others were probably thinking I needed to give it more thought. I was pretty set on it, even though it was possible I would regret my decision later on. My outward appearance would change and I understood that I needed to think thoroughly about how that would make me feel in the long term.

Maybe if this question had been put to me previously as a hypothetical one, I would have said hands down I would want a reconstruction. I would have looked at it through different eyes and been perhaps much more concerned about image.

There had been many times before that having a bad hair cut, or my stomach looking huge in a photo, or wearing the wrong outfit to an important event had seemed so catastrophic! How many times had I been so concerned about the timing of a large spot that appeared on my chin overnight or that the weighing scales showed I had put on two pounds that week? So if you had asked me a few months prior to discovering I had breast cancer what my thoughts would be about having my breasts removed, my reaction would have been much different.

When you are hit with an illness where you are uncertain about the outcome, things that you once thought were important suddenly seem so trivial – you are just so grateful to be alive. Times when I would have moaned about a nail chipping or I was wound up because too much hair was cut off my fringe suddenly didn't matter at all. I had a whole different perspective on things in life, and image was one of them.

Even though I was aware that my outward appearance would change and I imagined how not having breasts might make me feel as a woman, I had learned there were far more important things in life than how I looked. At that moment I was relieved that I was having treatment that would save my life. I think I was more eager to have the treatment and get rid of the cancer than to worry about mastectomy bras and clothes. I knew reconstruction was something I would consider again after I recovered, as I could always change my mind. Maybe in a year or two I would be in a better headspace to think about it.

It was 15 June and the day of my operation. Again, due to Covid-19, I had to go into hospital on my own. Family members were still not allowed to come with patients into hospitals. I was scared because I hadn't had a general anaesthetic before so I didn't know what to expect. I wanted Darren there to comfort and reassure me, and to be there when I woke up after the operation. He wanted to be there for me too, so dropping me off at the hospital that day was difficult for both of us. This was a big operation and I was facing more fears. As I got out of the car, walked through the doors of the hospital and waved goodbye to Darren, I reached and grabbed hold of the hand of Jesus once again, tight.

I first had to go to the radiology department to have some dye injected to highlight the main sentinel node. This was to enable the surgeon to take accurate biopsies during my operation. This was routine and the results would show whether I needed any further treatment following my operation.

It was a hot summer's day and I remember looking in the hospital mirror in the toilets after the surgeon had marked my body with a pen. There were arrows and markings to show him where to make incisions. As I stood there and looked at myself, I realized again that I was about to lose parts of my body and in a few hours I wasn't going to look the same. I knew this had to be done for the future and I needed to accept this and just 'be strong'. Walking down to the theatre with a nurse, I could feel my heart pounding. I was anxious about the anaesthetic and what it would feel like and I was aware of how big this operation was. However, I also had a picture that Jesus was already there waiting for me and, as I entered the anaesthetic room, even though I was faced with lots of machines and staff who were busily getting ready, I had a peace. The anaesthetist was lovely and put me at ease and as I lay on the bed with the sound of monitors around me, ready to be anaesthetized, in walked Barbara.

Barbara was a lady who attended our church. She worked as a theatre recovery nurse. As she walked in, my face lit up.

We were both so surprised to see one another. As I lay on the bed ready to be anaesthetized she bent beside me. I can't remember the exact things she said, but she whispered words of encouragement in my ear and reminded me that God was with me. God knew I needed a friendly face in that moment and sent Barbara in. Barbara ended up being my recovery nurse so she was there when I woke up too. What a gift she was! God surely was in every detail.

The operation went well and although I was understandably in pain for the following couple of months, I again was so thankful to Jesus for bringing me through it. A year or so on, even though it wasn't a pleasant thing to go through, I still don't regret not having reconstructions. I know there are women who make this decision and might not feel understood even by health professionals. I am grateful I had a very supportive breast surgeon who, although he took me through the whole process of reconstruction in detail, respected and understood my decision. There is an organization called 'Flat Friends' that supports women who have had to have a single or double mastectomy without breast reconstruction. I have included their website at the end of this book should any women wish to find out more about this source of support.

On 2 July, I had an appointment to discuss the results of the operation. As I mentioned, during the operation they had tested to see whether there were any cancer cells in my sentinel node. If there had been any present I might have needed radiotherapy and possibly more treatment. As I sat in the doctor's office he told me that the results were all clear and there had been only a couple of millimetres left of the cancer lump following the chemo. However, my breasts had been removed so this wasn't even a concern now. As the doctor told me this news, I sat there and my tears flowed. He told me to take a moment.

An overwhelming feeling of relief and gratitude just hit me. The breast nurse told me the oncologist didn't want to see me again, unless of course I ever needed to talk to him. I couldn't quite take it all in as I was so used to having more appointments.

All the requests that I had written on my Christmas gift tag in faith had been answered. God had heard my prayers.

That day, I walked out of the same hospital doors as I had gone through each time for my treatment, but this time I wasn't holding the hands of Jesus tight with fear – I was now swinging them with thankfulness.

I went on to have my ovaries and tubes removed on 30 December. I was under the care of such an amazing gynaecologist consultant, and on the recovery unit after my operation, I woke up to the lovely face of Barbara again. God had again positioned things with his mighty hands and I was aware of how he had gone before me.

My recovery went well. I had to wait to hear whether the ovaries and tubes were all clear of cancer; two weeks later I was told that everything removed was clear and so that marked the end of my treatment.

From the beginning of January 2021 right to the very end of December that year God had brought me through a journey that I had never thought I would ever go through. Through the ups and downs, he taught me so much and I knew my life wasn't going to be the same. Yes, I was tired, bruised and marked somewhat by the treatment but inside I felt renewed, changed and thankful that my life had been spared for a purpose. I recently went for my yearly check-up and was relieved that everything has settled well following my operations.

The word 'grateful' was one I said a lot during and after my treatment. I think I still use it most days now to sum up how I feel about everything. My brother and his wife gave me a framed picture as a gift that just had the word 'grateful' on it and nothing else, because they were aware I was saying it all the time! I don't think I understood what the word 'gratitude' really meant before, and now that I feel it, I can only describe it as a 'deep thankfulness'. It's a feeling that I wake up with daily that I can't really put into words. There are times even now when, out of nowhere, I find myself welling up with tears as my heart is so full of gratitude to Jesus.

## His Hands

When I got home after my last chemo, Abi was in Dudley with her fiancé and she sent me a picture of a double rainbow that had just appeared in the sky there. The rainbows stood bright against the dark, stormy-looking sky. A friend of ours also 'tagged me' in the same picture on social media. The timing of this was perfect – it was a reminder of God's promises and the hope we have in him. The fact it was a double rainbow made it even more special.

As we look at the colours of the rainbow we are reminded not only of the promises of God but also of how God's hands paint the picture. You see, he is God of the detail and was in every detail of my journey, and he is in every detail of your journey too. There is nothing that escapes him and there is nothing he doesn't see. He knows all the things you are concerned or scared about.

You may be in a storm right now in your own life but today I want to remind you that the promises of God still stand. What he says in his word about you and what you are facing is like those bright rainbows. They are a reminder that even though things may resemble a dark, stormy sky, his word, his name and his hands bring hope to any situation.

When I look back at the nurses, doctors and staff at the hospitals who looked after me, it was as though he put the right people for me in the right place at the right time. Even though it's not always this way in life, God knows us better than anyone and his hands can manoeuvre things on our behalf.

**Take a Moment . . .**

Why not make it a daily routine to be thankful for all that God has given you?

We don't often feel thankful when things are going wrong but having a constant, grateful heart keeps our hearts healthy.

Whatever you are going through right now, remember God is there with you.

He goes before you and will put things in place with his mighty hands.

# 12

# No Filter

When I kept that cold cap on throughout the first chemo treatment, I was so proud of myself. It was as though I had passed some sort of endurance challenge! Those first ten minutes were something else, but then I became used to it and it was bearable so I decided to try it again next time. However, about two or three weeks after the first treatment my hair started to fall out. I assumed the cold cap wasn't working for me, so I decided not to continue with it. I needed to resign myself to the fact that I was going to lose my hair – and losing your hair, particularly as a woman, is hard.

I had tried to grow my hair for my daughter's wedding and I had an expectation of how I wanted to look that day. Being the mother of the bride is something many women think about as their daughter grows up. They often have an image of how they would like to look for that special day. For the two years leading up to the wedding I lost count of the amount of times I declared I was on a diet! There was always a level of pressure, for me, that the mother of the bride needed to look her best, and part of achieving that goal was thinking of how I wanted my hair to look.

Generally, as women, we spend a lot of time (and money!) getting our hair the way we want it to look. When I think of the many haircuts I had while I was growing up, I have tried to embrace the on-trend styles throughout the decades – even though looking back at them I do wonder what I was thinking.

We really can put a lot of emphasis on image and we often don't even recognize we are doing so. It's a culture we have grown up in. I like fashion and to wear nice clothes and have my hair and make-up done, but I didn't think I was particularly hung up on those things. However, as I have mentioned, one of the first things I was distraught about when I knew about my chemo treatment was that I was going to be bald for Abi's wedding. Looking back, I now wonder why that was one of the first things that came out of my mouth. Not having any hair is something I guess a lot of women dread when they are about to have chemo treatment. Apart from the importance of what those drugs do to cancer, the effect it has on hair is also a well-known factor.

Our hair can be very much part of our identity and so when it's removed we can feel as though part of our identity is lost. I've had blonde highlights in my fair hair for as long as I can remember, so when my hair grew back it came through a darker colour than I remembered. When people initially saw me with this darker, short, cropped style they often didn't recognize me. They associated me with how I looked before, as my hair was part of my identity.

I held on to the fact that the cold cap might work for me although I knew the success of this was only 50/50. I had fine hair anyway so even if it thinned it would probably look like nothing, but even so I remember that day I realized the cold cap hadn't worked. My hair was starting to come out a lot. I don't know whether I was more disappointed that my endurance challenge hadn't succeeded or whether it was the realization of what was happening to me. I had blow-dried my hair and, as I sat there on the bed brushing it through, I watched my hair coming out in tufts on the brush. I looked at the mound of hair beside me on the bed and, as I looked at myself in the mirror, I cried. The hair-shedding continued over the next few days and, within a couple of weeks, I hardly had any hair left.

Although this was something I had been dreading, once it had come out I adjusted to it quickly. It was during the summer months and, as mentioned, we were in a lockdown so I wasn't really going anywhere anyway. I tried a number of wigs (which was another story in itself!) but I found wearing a sports cap much more comfortable and cooler. By the end of my treatment I had lost all my hair, but it wasn't so much of an issue to me as it had been at the start. Yes, I was looking forward to my hair growing back again, but I wasn't embarrassed in the way I had thought I was going to be. I had thought I would struggle and not want anyone to see me with no hair but, in reality, I was so thankful for life and that the treatment was working for me that 'image' seemed insignificant. I noticed that, generally, people assumed this was a greater problem for me than it actually was. I too would have thought this way before my diagnosis.

As I was recovering after my treatment, however, I started to reflect on what had happened to me. The numerous hospital appointments, procedures, treatments and operations had suddenly stopped and, although I welcomed this with open arms, I found myself now processing it all. It was almost as though I had been on a treadmill for a long time and I had suddenly jumped off, and was trying to get some equilibrium again.

All along, my family and friends were commenting on how well I coped with everything, but now that I had been given the all clear and the treatment had been completed, I think the reality of what I had been through started to sink in. I had handled the changes to my appearance well and, as I said previously, I didn't feel any differently towards my reconstruction decision. However, it took me a couple of weeks before I could properly look at my wounds in the mirror. They went from the middle of my body to under both of my arms. I knew they were there from the pain and stiffness I was experiencing, but looking at them almost made them more real to me – I found it easier if the area was covered up with my clothes.

This was a significant change. When I looked at myself in the mirror there was an obvious sign of something missing, and seeing that initially was difficult.

There was a moment one day when I realized that I had somewhat lost all those things that I thought made me a woman: I had no hair, no breasts and my ovaries were due to be removed.

To add to the sense of loss, a few weeks later my daughter Abi got married and left home; my son Jack had already left the year before for university. Those were exciting milestones for them. Although I was happy for them, I missed them so much in those early days, as any mother would. I had taken voluntary redundancy from the administration role I had as the department I worked for was doing a restructure. So, apart from my role with Aspire, I had lost my day job too. I had always been employed ever since leaving school so even though I needed a good rest, this was another big adjustment for me.

Many things had changed, and I felt stripped of who I was. I guess I felt the 'loss' and, as mentioned previously, with any loss, your heart hurts.

Before, I had been Leanne, who looked a certain way, a way that people identified me with. I had been mum at home to the kids. I had been busy in the day with my job. Now, in the sudden quietness of my home, I realized everything had changed. It was almost as though I was grieving a little for who I was, for my identity. Within a year things had changed so much that I struggled to know where I now fitted in.

I remember one day I had ordered outfits to try on for Abi's wedding. It wasn't long after my operation and I couldn't lift my arms very well. I got stuck in a dress trying to get it off. Nothing hung on me well any more. I just sat there and cried. I loved floral tops and pretty dresses but with no hair and no breasts I didn't feel feminine, and nothing seemed to suit me. Darren came in to help me out of my dress and to console me, and I cried in his arms. The reality of how different I now looked had hit me. This meltdown only happened once, because while I was crying, Darren reminded me how blessed I was to still be here, and the truth of that put everything in to perspective again very quickly.

Even now I still get moments of disappointment when I'm in a changing room looking at myself in clothes that just don't suit my shape any more, but now those frustrations really do fade into insignificance very quickly and are always replaced with overwhelming thankfulness for life.

Even though I struggled a little in those initial weeks, I didn't stay in that place for long. Focusing again on being thankful, I realized that, although things had changed outwardly, I was still the same Leanne. I was still a daughter to my parents, wife to Darren and mum to the kids. I needed a rest from working so I became actually very grateful for a recovery period and some time out. Yes, my physical body had changed, and my outlook on life had changed, but I was still that person God had formed in my mother's womb fifty-one years ago – my husband and my kids still loved me and the plan for my life was unchanged. I am so grateful for the endless support and love I had from my family that helped me to accept the changes I was adapting to.

Hearing some thoughts from my husband, I think, will help any spouses reading this, as so often a wife going through this type of treatment might need some extra reassurance. I also know that husbands might not get much opportunity to voice their concerns.

### Darren's thoughts . . .

It was so hard to watch my wife, Leanne, suffer and be stripped of what could feel like all her identity and image. There were times that I struggled keeping my emotions in but I always wanted to stay strong for her and my kids during this difficult period. As a pastor I'll be honest, I found it hard to pray at times because of how overwhelmed I felt, but I knew that God heard the cry of my heart even with the few words that I could sometimes muster. I believed that God would bring us through this tough season and bring healing to Leanne, but there were uncertainties along the way and these affected me at times.

Leanne was so strong, not only in her battle with breast cancer and through her treatment, but also dealing with the operations that were looming over her. As she was considering her options, I had questions myself: What would she go through? What would the operations entail? How would they do the mastectomies? I was given some literature initially from the hospital to help support those going through cancer but I still had questions of my own about the operation side of things. It was such a sensitive topic that I didn't want Leanne to feel I was being insensitive by bombarding her with lots of questions at a time when she had many of her own. Before Leanne explained to me how her body would look after the operation, I had my own image in my head of how they would do it and what it would look like. I had pictures of open wounds, and assumed it would be like this for her for some time. I was very surprised when I saw her after her operation, as it wasn't what I had imagined at all and it had been done so well.

I initially encouraged Leanne to consider reconstructions, as maybe I was too hung up on the image side myself and how this would affect her. Leanne is not a needy person, but would she feel differently about herself and need more reassurance from me after her operation? I didn't know how this was going to affect her, emotionally as well physically. I knew I needed to be more sensitive to her during this time.

As time went on, I could understand why she chose to not have reconstructions, and I respected her decision. Just having Leanne alive was more important. I realized things could have turned out a lot differently and I was so grateful to God for providing treatment and doctors that could save her life.

Leanne always took pride in the way she looked and I knew this would be difficult for her. I made sure that she knew that my love for her would not diminish even though she would look a bit different. To me, she is still the same Leanne that I fell in love with as a young boy and I married all those years ago: still beautiful inside and out and made in God's image.

When you marry someone, although you are attracted to them, you marry them for the person they are. Our physical bodies will change as we get older. When Leanne married me I had hair and when I lost that it didn't change her feelings towards me (at least, I don't think it did!).

I have come to realize that when we go through tough times some things aren't important any more. This last year has helped me re-evaluate my own life and what's important to me, and to us as a couple. It's helped us to put things into perspective.

Darren

I realize that in the days following my treatment and operation I was 'adjusting' rather than 'struggling'. I was able to accept what had happened to me fairly quickly because I realized my identity was actually in Christ and not in how I looked. When I made my decision to follow him all those years ago I accepted who he said I was. What he says about me and how he sees me is what I built my life on. 'Yet to all who did receive him, to those who believed in his name, he gave the right to become children of God' (John 1:12, NIV). When I made the decision to follow Jesus and made him the Lord of my life, this verse tells me that he gave me the right to become a child of God – and that is who I am. That is my identity.

Our names are important. When your birth is registered, there is a name attached to you. That name could change as you get married or if you change it by deed poll, but your name is your identity! Your passport carries a picture of you with your name underneath. Your name carries weight. When we sign mortgage documents or cheques, that signature has value. However, even though we have earthly parents and an earthly name at birth, the Bible says God knew us before we were even born.

For you created my inmost being;
>    you knit me together in my mother's womb.
I praise you because I am fearfully and wonderfully made;
>    your works are wonderful,
>    I know that full well.

(Ps. 139:13–14, NIV)

We all have a name that people identify us with, but our identity goes right back to before we were even born and named by our parents. God knew us even then, and so what God says about us is who we are. Our identity comes from him who made us.

The way I looked had changed but it didn't affect me perhaps as other people thought it would, because actually the things that are the bedrock of who I am haven't changed at all. God's word tells me who I am and that is unchanged.

Often we base our identity on things that don't actually make us who we are. Society will say your job, the way you look, your title, your status are who you are. Remember when I drenched myself in water before stepping up to the platform to speak? It reminded me that image, titles and roles are not important and it was a valuable lesson that stayed with me.

We can so often base our identity and worth on what others think of us and we can waste so much of our time chasing after those things. We feel we have to be accepted by those we think are important or popular and that is what will give us credibility and value. You see, what usually happens is that people let us down, jobs come and go, titles can be taken away. If we have based our worth on those things, in those people, we will travel through life feeling constantly hurt and offended as situations change.

In autumn 2022, the nation mourned the sad passing away of Queen Elizabeth II. As we watched her funeral on TV and saw the crown on top of her coffin, I am sure we were all hit with the realization that no matter whether we are a king or queen, we will all leave this earth one day. Queen Elizabeth was aware of her title here on earth and the role that she had, and she served that well; but among the many things she has said over the years, clearly what was important to her was her faith in God. She knew that one day she would meet with her Maker, and titles, earthly crowns and jewels would be stripped away. You see, she too knew the importance of being a child of God and *that* title, at the end of her life, remained. The Bible reminds us of how we come into the world and how we will leave it: 'For we brought nothing into the world, and we can take nothing out of it' (1 Tim. 6:7, NIV).

Today, because I know I am still God's child, still his daughter, that he still loves me, I'm still forgiven, still accepted and he still calls me his own – that makes me secure in who I am. That knowledge of who I am will never change. What a comfort and security that is! If I had based my identity on what the world says is important, I would perhaps have struggled a whole lot more. It was yet another moment when I realized the importance of building my life on the rock.

God's word tells us that when we come to Christ we are new and we are his child. God's word also tells us that we are forgiven – that is who we are!

Therefore, if anyone is in Christ, the new creation has come: the old has gone, the new is here!

(2 Cor. 5:17, NIV)

I have been crucified with Christ and I no longer live, but
Christ lives in me. The life I now live in the body, I live by faith
in the Son of God, who loved me and gave himself for me.

(Gal. 2:20, NIV)

See what great love the Father has lavished on us, that we
should be called children of God! And that is what we are!
The reason the world does not know us is that it did not
know him.

(1 John 3:1, NIV)

If we confess our sins, he is faithful and just and will forgive
us our sins and purify us from all unrighteousness.

(1 John 1:9, NIV)

The way we look at situations that happen to us in life makes
all the difference to how we go forward. It's the same for
the way we can look at disappointment. We have a choice.
When I look at my scars now I see them as reminders of being
healed, reminders of what Jesus has brought me through. A
mother who has stretch marks after carrying her baby for nine
months can look at them either as marks on her body that she
needs to hide because she now perceives herself as flawed, or
as reminders of the wonderful gift she has been given: each
mark represents how amazing her body is in giving birth to
her child. It's your perception of what has happened that matters and this will determine your steps going forward. Absurd
though it sounds, I am grateful for my scars – marks that show
the incredible work of our doctors and how truly amazing my
God is.

Talking about how God is in the detail of things – and how I always wanted my hair to be for Abi's wedding – I eventually found a wig that gave me the exact look I had envisaged. Even though image wasn't a priority to me, God knew that my daughter's wedding was important for me. I don't think my natural hair would ever have given me what I had pictured, but amazingly this wig did.

Regarding what clothes I can or cannot wear now – the Bible clearly tells me not to worry about those things either:

> And why do you worry about clothes? See how the flowers of the field grow. They do not labour or spin. Yet I tell you that not even Solomon in all his splendour was dressed like one of these. If that is how God clothes the grass of the field, which is here today and tomorrow is thrown into the fire, will he not much more clothe you – you of little faith?
> (Matt. 6:28–30, NIV)

At the end of my treatment, when I went on to social media to give God thanks as I had said I would, I posted a picture of me with no hair. People commented how brave I was to do this but this was who I was in that moment and I wanted to make a strong statement that we shouldn't be embarrassed by how we look just because it isn't perceived as the norm. This was a reality for me and if I couldn't post a picture of what I looked like because of what people might think, it would be extremely sad.

Our theme for the Aspire women's ministry over the last couple of years had been 'Be Real'. We recognized a few years ago the importance of being our real and authentic selves as women. Being vulnerable about the things we struggle with. Being real before both others and God releases us in so many ways. We wanted to send a message out to say, 'It's OK to be real.'

In Scripture, we read about how being real before God is also important for our lives:

Don't be pulled in different directions or worried about a thing. Be saturated in prayer throughout each day, offering your faith-filled requests before God with overflowing gratitude. Tell him every detail of your life, then God's wonderful peace that transcends human understanding, will guard your heart and mind through Jesus Christ. Keep your thoughts continually fixed on all that is authentic and real, honorable and admirable, beautiful and respectful, pure and holy, merciful and kind. And fasten your thoughts on every glorious work of God, praising him always.

(Phil. 4:6–9, TPT)

This passage speaks about how we should keep our thoughts on things that are authentic and real. God is interested in every part of our lives and he wants us to talk to him about all of it. He knows what we think anyway so there is no reason why we can't be real before him.

I needed to demonstrate, by posting a picture of myself bald, that this was real for me, and this is OK. I don't think I could have dreamt of posting something like that before, but my outlook on life after going through this cancer journey has changed.

I am increasingly aware that, on social media, celebrities, models and influencers are posting pictures of themselves with a hashtag and the words 'no filter'. They are all recognizing that this generation wants authenticity, they are looking for 'real'. When a filter is applied, it's almost admitting that the real person, in their raw form, isn't enough. We can all compare ourselves with the body of the model that we see advertising a beach holiday, and then feel we must cover up as we don't match up to the expectation.

Adverts with models advertising beauty products, face creams and fragrances are edited to a standard that make them look more vibrant and flawless than they are. Yet society is starting to realize that this is not reality, and people are not getting sucked in to this marketing strategy. It's becoming popular now for women, even models, to be real and admit their pictures are edited, by showing pictures of how they really look alongside the edited version. Clothing brands are starting to use models of all shapes and sizes, and society is welcoming this more and more. We have to model to the next generation that we are beautiful no matter how we look and there isn't a standard, flawless look that we should compare ourselves to.

For my daughter, Abi, a woman in her early twenties, image may be of more importance than for me at my age. Watching her mum navigate these changes taught her some life lessons and so I thought it would be good for Abi to share her thoughts on this whole subject of image and identity as a young woman.

### Abi's thoughts . . .

When Mum was diagnosed as having breast cancer, I think one of the things which I had never thought of until it started to happen was the fact that I had to watch her go through such a gruelling treatment. Chemo took away her hair and her energy, and her day-to-day life completely changed within weeks. She couldn't go anywhere due to Covid-19. She had to have cycles of strong chemo which left her weak and made her hair fall out. She had to have her breasts and her ovaries removed.

I watched my mum be so strong during those times. She is a fighter and I'm so proud of her; but I also watched moments of sadness and loss. As a daughter that was such a hard time, because all I wanted was to make it go away and to take the pain away from her. When your mum is the 'fixer' all your life . . . it's almost as if our roles reversed when she started going through this period, and I wanted to be the 'fixer' for her. However, I knew that I couldn't fix this in my own strength.

This season of my life taught me a lot about not only trusting in God and trusting he has full control over our lives, but also how we are made in God's image and how our identity is in him. Mum is beautiful because she is made in God's image; that never changed. Though it was tough seeing her go through this experience, it taught me a lot. I really felt God was teaching me during this time that whatever fades in life, God and our identity in him remains constant and will never leave us. We can lose hair, lose bits of our bodies, lose a ton of different physical attributes on earth, but we can never ever lose God or his love for us and who he has called us to be. That is definitely something I will take forward with me forever and continue to remember now that Mum's better. The world can try to steal and convince us that our earthly image is everything, but it's really not. All I wanted was for Mum to be better, and I think going through something like this as a family teaches you that the things you worried about before, do not matter. You just want those that you love to be well again.

I value life differently now. I view image completely differently. I take in each moment more. As Mum had the altered BRCA 1 gene, I am about to embark on testing to see if I have it and, though this brings about uncertainty for me, I have a peace knowing that regardless what that shows, God's plans for my life will not change. He made me in his image and I can trust that regardless of whether that faulty gene is in my body or not – my mum taught me that!

What I will say is to those who are watching parents or loved ones going through a similar journey: it isn't easy and often you feel so helpless and you just want to make it better for them. There is often a lot of loss and a feeling of unfairness that comes with this battle. Cancer is cruel and the treatment literally almost strips a person, but know that God's identity lives in you and them and that, no matter what, God's plan is higher, and greater. Our flesh and bones may fade away but our soul is what's important – I definitely view that as the main priority in my life now.

My prayer as I looked forward to my wedding was that my mum would be there, cancer-free, and we would sing out about the goodness of God. I thank God that as I looked over to her on my wedding day I could give thanks that my prayer had been answered.

Abi

## His Hands

I don't think we are created by God's hands to then hide away because we don't fit in to a box that society has created. However, even though we are generally now recognizing this as a cultural feature, I think we can become part of the solution in helping others to be who God created them to be, by being authentic and real ourselves. Verses in Psalm 139, Psalm 119 and Ephesians remind us that his hands have created us and his hands don't make mistakes.

> For you created my inmost being;
>     you knit me together in my mother's womb.
> I praise you because I am fearfully and wonderfully made;
>     your works are wonderful,
>     I know that full well.
>
> > (Ps. 139:13–14, NIV)

> Your hands made me and formed me;
>     give me understanding to learn your commands.
>
> > (Ps. 119:73, NIV)

> For we are God's handiwork, created in Christ Jesus to do good works, which God prepared in advance for us to do.
>
> > (Eph. 2:10, NIV)

God created and made you for purpose – you are his 'handiwork'. If we struggle with accepting this then we need to allow the Holy Spirit to work in us to reform the way we think. This verse in Romans tells us that we can live a beautiful life, not a life spent comparing ourselves to others, but living a life with a knowledge that we are perfect in his eyes: 'Stop imitating the ideals and opinions of the culture around you, but be inwardly transformed by the Holy Spirit through a total reformation of how you think. This will empower you to discern God's will as you live a beautiful life, satisfying and perfect in his eyes' (Rom. 12:2, TPT).

**Take a Moment . . .**

Are you constantly comparing yourself to others?

Are you looking for acceptance in all the wrong places?

Understanding that God created you with his mighty hands, and he sees you as perfect, should be enough.

Romans 12 talks about 'being inwardly transformed by the Holy Spirit through a total reformation of how you think'. If you struggle with how you see yourself, maybe ask the Holy Spirit today to reform how you think.

You are his child, he created you and his works are wonderful – you are enough!

When he made you, you were 'beautifully and wonderfully made'. Being secure in what God says about us will release us in so many ways and will enable us to live a life of freedom and acceptance.

# 13

# Moving On

Each one of us has been through tough seasons in our lives. Many reading this have experienced health battles, loss and heartache. None of us would choose to go through such times due to the pain and hurt they bring. However, it's important we look for what we learned through them so that we can not only take those lessons forward with us, but also can help others facing similar paths. There were many lessons I learned through my health battle that have changed my life in such a positive way. I am certainly not the same person I was a year ago and I wanted to end this book just highlighting some of these things that I will take with me into the days ahead.

I realize that there will be a time of restoration for me now as I recover and I want to give time to God to heal not only my physical body from the after-effects but also my emotions too. When you go through a traumatic experience it's good to allow yourself time for God to heal you in every area of your life. God is a God of restoration and, when we go through tough times and feel battle-weary, his desire is to restore us.

My prayer is that sharing how I plan to move forward with what I have learned will encourage you to focus on what really matters in life. When you are faced with something that brings uncertainty, it can change your whole outlook on things. I now feel I have an opportunity to assess areas of my life that need to change, so that I may not only live the full life that Jesus talks about, but also make sure I am living with purpose.

## My time

We can become so busy with life in general that we can often neglect the things or people that are really important to us. Going through breast cancer, I noticed there were many things that I used to think were important that actually weren't at all. I am finding I'm far more chilled and laid back as I recover and I am cherishing the slower pace of life for me right now. I realize that things will pick up for me again soon but as I have this time to reflect on life I really want to get things right going forward.

Before my diagnosis, life was pretty busy. I was balancing a day job, leading a ministry, I was a pastor's wife and a mum. People would often ask me how I was doing it all and, in all honesty, I'm not sure I was balancing everything well. I described it as spinning many plates but it often felt as though I was just running around, keeping them barely spinning. I needed to reflect on it all and this time made me do just that. I could take a step back from life and fully see what needed to change going forward.

**My perspectives and priorities**

One thing that has changed is the way I react to things. Things that used to annoy me or get a reaction from me just don't bother me as much. I try to steer away from gossip and negativity too as I want to protect my heart and what I allow in even more than I did before. Don't get me wrong, I'm human – so I will no doubt still have my buttons pushed but it's almost as though there is a check there now that reminds me of what is important in life and what is not worth getting stressed or angry about.

There was one situation I was faced with after my treatment that I perhaps would have been expected to be really cross and hurt over previously, but my outlook had changed so much that my response was to quickly let it go. I was able to quite happily discharge it and move on. I'm not saying I don't feel disappointment or hurt, but my reaction to it has somewhat changed.

When a storm hits your life and you are uncertain whether you are going to survive it, many things are put in perspective. You find yourself thinking: if I get through this I'll change this, I'll change that, I'll never think that way again, I won't get stressed at petty things again and I'll make certain areas of my life a priority – almost longing for a second chance to put things right and in the right order. It can be so easy then to forget those things when everything is OK and you have a different mindset. It's as though I have had a step back from life and can appreciate the beauty of it. I am more aware now that we do have a choice with how we fill our hearts and our minds and I want to get it right now. I find myself guarding my heart more than ever. I'm careful about my choices now and who I surround myself with. I guess I feel so blessed to have another chance at life that I want to honour God more and, even though I am far from perfect, I want to make sure I'm right before him.

Throughout my treatment, I became so close to God, closer than I probably have ever felt before. I almost didn't want to get back to the busyness of life again as I would miss those precious times. This was something I really wanted to protect. The fast pace of life, fulfilling all my roles might prevent spending enough time with the one I serve. It's like being a mum and doing all the chores 24/7 for your children, but spending no quality time with them and not enjoying your precious gifts. I think every mum knows the frustration of that. I now have a second chance of putting this right and I want to make sure it's more of a priority going forward – that I'm never too busy again to enjoy life and to appreciate the beauty of it and enjoy special times with my heavenly Father.

In our busyness we can often neglect spending time with our family too. I know this isn't always easy if you don't live near each other but making quality time with them is something I learned is important. When things seemed to be being stripped away from me, God and my family were what I appreciated and clung on to more than anything. Those were the things that really mattered to me. I find myself taking more time to show how important people are to me now too. When family birthdays or Christmas come around I am finding I want to show how much they mean to me more, whether it's a soppy social media post or showering people with gifts. It's just something I naturally want to do because I appreciate them so much more.

As I travelled this journey the way I looked, my jobs, the house and money just slowly started to seem insignificant. We can put so much emphasis and attention on these things. Yes, we need a job, a home and money to live, and it's OK to want to look our best, but these things can easily get put in the wrong place on our priority list and our lives can get out of balance so quickly. Through this time, I got to know what was important very clearly and so going forward I don't want to forget those lessons. As previously mentioned, knowing who you are in Christ makes all the difference when your world turns upside down. Life is full of unexpected changes but choosing to build your life on him ensures that the most important things in your life will never change.

**My fears**

I learned that, even if we are faced head-on with our fears, Jesus carries us in the storm. In the Gospel of Matthew we read the story of when Jesus was with his disciples and he was asleep on the boat. The disciples started to panic when a storm hit them and this was Jesus' response: "'You of little faith, why are you so afraid?" Then he got up and rebuked the winds and the waves, and it was completely calm' (Matt. 8:26, NIV). I'm sure Jesus wants to ask us the same question when we get into a state of panic. There were moments along my journey where fear started to set in, but I had to remember, when things seemed out of my control, that he was in total control.

As I mentioned at the start, I used to be very fearful, and every pain I had I imagined was something terrible. One of those fears became a reality, and this journey with cancer has made me realize that 'even if' we are faced with our fears we can be assured the Lord will comfort us.

In the Bible there are Scriptures that remind us that 'even though' or 'even if' we find ourselves in the valley, 'even though' everything seems against us and 'even though' things don't turn out as we expect . . . we don't need to fear, we can still be confident and we can still rejoice in him – as he gives us strength.

> Even though I walk
>     through the darkest valley,
> I will fear no evil,
>     for you are with me;
> your rod and your staff,
>     they comfort me.

                                        (Ps. 23:4, NIV)

Though an army besiege me,
   my heart will not fear;
though war break out against me,
   even then I will be confident.

(Ps. 27:3, NIV)

Even though the fig trees have no blossoms,
   and there are no grapes on the vines;
even though the olive crop fails,
   and the fields lie empty and barren;
even though the flocks die in the fields,
   and the cattle barns are empty,
yet I will rejoice in the LORD!
   I will be joyful in the God of my salvation!
The Sovereign LORD is my strength!
   He makes me as surefooted as a deer,
   able to tread upon the heights.

(Hab. 3:17–19, NLT)

What a comfort this is that 'even if' or 'even though' . . . he is still with us. Even if you are faced with your worst fear. Even if! God will be right by your side. Some responses we have are natural, but experiencing how close he was to me during my storm, how he held my hand, and knowing how powerful his name is, brings a comfort and assurance that I know has changed how I think and react to situations.

**My soul**

We read in the Bible that Job had his fair share of suffering – how Job reacts to what happened to him is something I think we can all learn from too. Here is a man who loses almost everything – his sheep, his oxen, and his sons and daughters had terrible things happen to them – but through it all he didn't lose his faith in God. We read his response in the book of Job: '"Naked I came from my mother's womb, and naked I shall depart. The LORD gave and the LORD has taken away; may the name of the LORD be praised." In all this, Job did not sin by charging God with wrongdoing' (Job 1:21–2, NIV).

In life, the Lord gives and the Lord takes away. We can all give an account of someone or something in our lives that we have lost. We can struggle with that; the pain of that can hurt deeply. We can equally, I'm sure, give an account of times when we have received what we could describe as 'blessings from above', whether that's the gift of children, job promotion, a spouse or a house. Many if not all of us have experienced the joy of the 'added things' but also the heartache of the 'taking away', and Job here in this verse acknowledges both, but praises God. Again, Job recognizes that he came into this world with nothing and he will leave with nothing. We came into this world naked and there will be nothing we will need from this world when we depart.

One of my favourite hymns is 'It is Well with My Soul' by Horatio Spafford, and sung with music composed by Philip Paul Bliss. I remember when I was a child they used to sing it at our church in Cardiff and as they sang the powerful words they would wave their hymn books in the air and sing it from the depths of their hearts. I don't love this hymn only because of the great words and music arrangement; the story behind why it was written really makes the words seem so much more powerful.

A man called Horatio suffered much loss – his businesses, his son aged only four years, and then his four daughters at sea. He lost just about everything that was precious to him. When Horatio sailed past the point at sea where his daughters had died, he penned the words to his hymn.

When peace like a river, attendeth my way,
When sorrows like sea billows roll
Whatever my lot, thou hast taught me to say
It is well, it is well, with my soul.

His words were basically saying that whatever life had thrown at him, the good and bad, what mattered was that it was well with his soul. His heart must have been broken, but he knew what mattered in life.

We may have questions about why we feel loved ones were taken from us too early. We may not know why the timing of these things happen and won't know those answers until we meet with him in eternity, but what we do know is that God holds our future in his hands. Psalm 31:15 reminds us that: 'My times are in your hands'.

Horatio expressed in those difficult moments that what really mattered was his soul. What happens here on earth is temporary. As previously mentioned, we will all move on from this earth at some point and where we will spend eternity does matter. Making sure our soul is well is all that matters when everything is stripped away. When I felt some areas of my life had been stripped away, what helped me accept it quickly was not just a new perspective on life, but because I had a peace in my heart knowing that Jesus was with me. This was my bedrock and that's what gave me the biggest comfort and strength through the uncertainty. If the outcome had been different with my diagnosis and the treatment hadn't been as successful,

I still could have declared that it was well with my soul – and that is all that would have mattered. 'For I am convinced that neither death nor life, neither angels nor demons, neither the present nor the future, nor any powers, neither height nor depth, nor anything else in all creation, will be able to separate us from the love of God that is in Christ Jesus our Lord' (Rom. 8:38–9, NIV).

## His Hands

The moment I think I really started to notice what the Lord's hands were doing in my situation was one Saturday night, at the beginning of my chemo treatment. I was watching a Saturday night TV programme. One of the celebrities on the show sang a well-known song called 'With These Hands' that was once sung by Elvis! The words of the song, however, really stood out to me. Although it isn't a Christian song, as soon as I heard it, it was as though the Lord was pointing out what his hands could do for me and how he would never let go of me.

Through the appointments, scans, procedures and results I had, he was there holding my hand. There were times I needed his hand to hold. There were times his hands led me through the doors of the hospital. Times when he picked me up and just held me. Times his hands surrounded me and held me close. His hands would provide for me, and what a comfort that was. I never thought God would minister to me so powerfully through such a secular song – but it made me smile. For each appointment and chemo treatment I would grab his hands as I went through the doors of the hospital, and I never once felt alone.

On a recent Mother's Day here in the UK, social media was plastered with pictures of mothers and words of appreciation. However, one particular picture caught my eye. Someone had posted a picture of her mother's hands. The picture seemed to capture why her mother meant so much without saying a word. Looking at those hands, even though they had now somewhat aged, probably conjured up so many memories for her: the way her mother used her hands to cook for her, put on plasters, brush her hair, clean her room, drive her to places, wipe her tears, tuck her up in bed and hold her hand when she was scared. In that one photograph was a complete picture of a mother's love.

If I look at my parents' hands today, I know them well – I would recognize their hands anywhere! They are hands that have comforted me, provided and cared for me. As a child there were no better hands to be in as they protected me and were my comfort. Often a tiny baby can cry when they are not in their mother's or father's arms. It's amazing that even though they are so small they recognize and know Mum and Dad and can stop crying when they are back in their arms. It's a comfort to them.

There were times while I was growing up when we would notice how my hands were like my dad's hands; the shapes of my nails and fingers were just like his. Isn't that a picture of how we, as God's children, must resemble the hands of Jesus – that he wants us to be his hands and feet in the world today? That through what we do for people and the way we care, people would see him. We can show his love in action. It's a challenge to us all that we look at our hands and ask whether others can see Jesus in us.

Just as I would recognize my mum's or dad's hands if I saw them in a picture, I think of the hands of Jesus now when I recognize what he has done for me. I've got to know his hands – the way he has provided, loved and cared for me. Looking back over my life and recognising how he gently took my hand to show me what he could do in and through me was key for me in the way I trusted his hands in this season. What we mean to him is proved by looking at his hands. Jesus' hands were nailed to a cross for us – that is how much he loves us.

The other week, I took my daughter Abi to have her genetic test. It was something that she knew she needed to have done but which she was in no hurry to do. As I carry the faulty BRCA 1 gene, it was advised that members of my family should be tested. This was a positive step for them, because if they did carry the gene they could be monitored more closely and things can be put in place to prevent or reduce the risks of them having cancer. Even though it's something that perhaps they didn't want to discover, I wanted to reassure them all that knowing this would only benefit them. If I had known I carried this gene earlier, I would have taken steps to prevent myself going through all that I had the year before. I often think that maybe by going through this, it has resulted in many of my family – my children, my future grandchildren, my nieces, cousins and their children – being monitored and prevented from getting cancer in the future, and that is surely a positive thing. I am so thankful for the ongoing developments with genetics and the discoveries and breakthroughs that are happening all the time to help prevent diseases occurring later on in life.

There was a 50 per cent chance of Abi carrying the altered gene and a simple blood test would tell her. We arrived at the hospital and tried to find our way to the genetics department. The hospital has many buildings and finding our way was proving difficult. A nurse came by and she could see we were lost. Even though there was going to be quite a long walk she offered to take us there and began to lead the way. I mentioned that my daughter was only there for a blood test that day and after hearing that she stopped in her tracks and said we didn't need to walk over to genetics but could have the test right there in the department where we were. Abi was called through almost immediately and the nurse who was taking the blood was asking lots of questions regarding the test, so that it could be sent to the right place.

As I stood there chatting to the nurse, giving her all the information I had, I watched her taking Abi's blood sample. The nurse then explained that we needed to take the sample over to the genetics building ourselves. I thought this was a bit strange at first, as usually this is done internally in hospitals, and so after an initial inside sigh that we actually had to do the long walk in the end, I felt a real challenge starting to rise up in me. As I watched the tube fill with blood, I realized that we would have Abi's blood in our hands and we would be taking it ourselves to be tested. When do you ever carry your blood test direct to the lab? I started to well up with tears at the realization that this was something significant. I wasn't sure whether Abi carried the faulty gene or not but, if she did, could I believe that God would change the picture again? I didn't want Abi to go through breast cancer, and so what was I going to do about what was in my hands? This was just a sample of her blood but to me it represented her.

We didn't really mind that we had to walk a fair distance to the lab as we had time to pray! Through my tears I declared that God was our healer, and prayed that day that the genetic line stopped with me, that the faulty gene would be stopped in its tracks. We knew this was a significant moment and we both held the tube together as we prayed. We handed the test over with a faith that God had heard our prayers and seen the faith we had.

About a month later, Abi rang me as she had received a letter from the hospital. The letter stated that there was (in big letters) NO EVIDENCE of the BRCA 1 alteration detected in her. The words that followed were: 'As you have not inherited the BRCA 1 gene alteration, you cannot pass it to any children you have.' There surely were a few tears that day as we thanked God together.

My prayer is that, even if any of my family tests positive with this faulty gene, the alteration now stops with them and that this is something that doesn't affect any of our children or children's children.

In life, there will always be situations or circumstances that we are presented with that seem set in stone, immovable. I like to think of them as things that are 'in our hands'. Not that we have any control over the outcome, but how we look at these things *is* in our hands. Can we have mustard seed-sized faith that God can turn it around? Can we believe that he can change the mountain-type problems that we face?

The other morning I woke up from a dream. The dream seemed to have lasted just a few seconds and it was just as I woke up so it was on my mind instantly. In my dream I was in a netball match and I had been thrown the ball. In my hands I held the ball and so what happened next in that game was up to me. What I did with that ball was now in 'my hands'. I knew when I woke up that this dream was for a point in my book, but I didn't quite know what it meant or where it would fit in, so I have been waiting for God to show me. Today, it hit me that I have had another chance at life and it's as though the ball has been thrown to me again and what happens next is in my hands. I want to make my life count and I want to serve God wholeheartedly. However, I am asking these questions: What am I doing with the things he has placed in my hands? Am I faithful with those things? Am I appreciating what I have been given? Am I just accepting things are as they are, or am I believing God can do the impossible or unexpected and turn things around? Am I using my gifts enough for him? Am I a witness for him to those in my sphere of influence?

As I have given my life to Jesus, I know that my next steps are ordered by him, and I want to make sure my next moves are in tune with his and keep that sat nav on.

There have been many challenges in this book and perhaps as you have read this you have been handed a 'ball of opportunity' to come to Jesus. What you do with that is now in your hands, but if you choose to place your 'ball' in the hands of the Almighty you will live the fullest, most purposeful life and not only that but when you leave this earth, you'll have the assurance that you will walk right into his arms.

I can't thank God enough for what he brought me through, and I'm sure many reading this will feel the same about their lives. Even in the tough times or when things don't turn out as expected, he is still God and he is still good. Life has its ups and downs because things here on earth are not perfect but just know that there is one thing that is constant and that is . . . his love endures forever, and for that we give thanks.

Give thanks to the LORD, for he is good;
    his love endures for ever.

(Ps. 107:1, NIV)

Recently at a conference I heard a song by Elim Sound called, 'I Have a Saviour'.[4] As I sang the song a couple of the verses resonated with me as they reflected some of my feelings after coming through this season of my life. I want to end this book leaving you with those words. I want to remind you that whatever you are going through today, you are not forgotten and you have a Saviour who carries your cares with 'his hands'.

'Cause I have walked through the wilderness
I've been crushed by the weight of my fears
But I'm not forgotten
I will trust in Your Word
'Cause I have a Saviour who carries my cares
I've been down,
I've been down on my knees, crying out to You God
But this I know,
If there's a miracle or not, You're still a good God
If there's a miracle or not, You're still a good God.

**Take a Moment . . .**

If you have reached the end of this book, I want first to thank you for the time you have spent in reading my story. I realize that our stories continue being written and I pray that some of what I have learned so far will have encouraged you in your journey too.

Maybe take a few moments before reaching out for your next book and ask God, is there a reason this book is in my hands at this moment?

Whether you know me and were interested to hear my story, or whether you were given this book to read by someone, or even stumbled across this book when searching for something else – maybe God wanted to speak to you about your life today. Maybe there is something in this book that he wanted to remind you of.

In Isaiah 49:16 the Lord says, 'I have engraved you on the palms of my hands.' That is how much he loves you and how much you mean to him.

I pray that you will not only close this book encouraged but will close it knowing the next chapter of your life is about to be written too.

If you don't know Jesus today, why not accept the invitation to make him your Lord and Saviour by praying the prayer below – it will be the best decision of your life – his hand is outstretched ready for you!

> Lord Jesus, I come before you now and accept you as Lord over my life. Thank you for dying on the cross for me and please forgive me, Jesus, for all the things I have done wrong. Please come into my heart right now and fill me with your Holy Spirit. Thank you for saving me and help me, Lord, to follow in your ways all the days of my life. Amen.

# Resources

If you have been encouraged by reading my story or you want to know more about God, I would love to hear from you. Please go to my website at www.leannemallett.com and fill out the contact page.

**Websites for further advice, help and support for breast cancer**

Breastcancernow.org
Macmillan.org.uk
Cancerresearchuk.org

**If you are wanting support regarding reconstructions following mastectomies**

Flatfriends.org.uk

**If you feel isolated or need someone to talk to**

Please contact your local GP, a hospital or church in your area. They can also signpost you to many other organizations in your area that can help you.

The Samaritans are also a great organization if you need to talk to someone. They can be contacted by dialling 116 123 or by going to their website: www.samaritans.org

**Other charity organizations mentioned**

The Elim Church
www.elim.org.uk

**If you are going through a health battle of any kind or suffering from pain**

Eric Gaudion has written a book called, *Through the Storms: A Manual for When Life Hurts* (Rickmansworth: Instant Apostle, 2020). His website is www.through-the-storms.com

# Thank Yous

There are so many people I want to thank for the way they supported me through my breast cancer journey. Your love and support meant so much to me. This book is dedicated to my Heavenly Father for all he has done in my life. However, I wanted to also dedicate this section to thanking those without whom my journey would have been much tougher.

### Darren – my husband

Thank you for always being a rock to me, for giving me support and space and just loving me through this. I know this turned your world upside down too for a little while but you kept strong for me and your calmness gave me so much comfort. I know this was hard for you too, as due to the pandemic you couldn't be by my side in any appointments, operations and treatments. I knew you had many questions and uncertainties but your faith in God kept you strong and I'm so thankful he was your strength and comfort through this too. You respected my decisions, and I already knew that whatever I chose to do regarding my operations, you would stand by me.

Thank you for allowing me to rest and recover, and never once trying to hurry that process along. You kept the house going with all your cleaning (I know how much you love cleaning, so it wasn't too much of a chore!) and I want you to know how much I appreciated everything you did for me. You never grumbled once even though you were sleeping in the spare room for six months! So I just want to say how much I love you and value all your love and care, as always.


**Abi – my daughter**

You walked this journey with me and were there for me every step of the way. This wasn't what you envisaged for the lead-up to your wedding, I know, but you were so strong for me. I am so grateful you had support from your now husband, and my now son-in-law, Luke. I want to thank you too, Luke – thank you for being there for Abi. I know it wasn't easy at times but knowing that you were there for her meant so much to me. Thank you too for your prayers (and patience!) when you were trying to plan for your wedding. I owe you many sticky toffee puddings!

Abi – you mentioned that on your wedding day, you just wanted me there, free of cancer. You wanted a moment at the wedding where we could look at each other as we sang about the goodness of God. I thank God we had that moment, that look, that smile, that acknowledgement as we sang and I will never forget the realization that day of how faithful God had been. You stood shoulder to shoulder with me not only as a daughter but also as a friend, and I cannot express my thanks enough. You could tell on which days I was struggling and would always say something that lifted me up or encouraged me. To see your faith in God grow during this time was just incredible, and lovely for any mum to see. You became my prayer warrior and often when I was at the hospital having chemo, appointments or scans you would be praying fervently at home for me. The determination and strength that I saw as you fought for your life as a premature baby, I saw again through this time. Thank you for being a rock to me too. Keep trusting in God all the days of your life, and keep being the lovely, gentle person you are. I'm so proud of you and I love you so much. Thank you, Abs.

**Jack – my son**

You are not only loved by me and your family, but you are such a good, loyal friend to all those around you, and that is what you were like to me through this journey too. Growing up, you would often share words of wisdom about a situation when we would least expect it, and it would often stop us in our tracks. One teacher in secondary school used to call you 'Jack genius', as you were known for coming out with things that were, at times, just genius!

Jack, you had a confidence throughout my treatment that was a comfort and strength to me. You felt all the way through that I would be OK and, even though at the start you were concerned and had questions, once you understood the situation you were confident I was in the best hands. I knew you were praying for me too, Jack, and had confidence in God. I want to thank you for being that rock to me too. There were often times when I would go into your bedroom and start up conversations that allowed me to answer any worries or concerns you might have but didn't voice. I am not totally convinced you had many of those questions but it made me feel better that I was reassuring you anyway. You know how much I like to chat to you! That same confidence you had in God during my health battle, always remember, is in the same God who is with you all the days of your life. Keep believing in him and keep putting him in the centre of all your decisions. Keep being that happy, funny, sensitive person we all know you for. I am so proud of you too and love you lots and lots. Thank you, boi.

## Jacqui and Nigel – my mum and dad

I was so grateful for you both and all you did for me throughout my treatment. The sacrificial love you both showed I have seen throughout my life in the way you have cared and loved me. You have always been there for me while I was growing up. A particular memory is of a sports event at primary school. Parents had been invited to come and watch if they wanted to and on this occasion you were the only parents who turned up. It was a shame I wasn't sporty and didn't bring in any gold medals that day but the memory makes me chuckle because you were treated like royalty as you were the only parents there – and that level of support and love has never stopped, even to this day. Thank you that you came and lived with us during my treatment and through those pandemic months, helping us in practical ways. I know it was hard seeing me go through this but I know you wouldn't have wanted it any other way than to be with me. Anyone who knows you knows that you give everything to serve others. The way you always put others first is something that has been modelled and demonstrated to me in many ways while I was growing up.

## Mum

Thanks, Mum, for doing my injections into my stomach at the beginning of every cycle. Again, not an easy job and I think it hurt you more than it hurt me, but you made a great nurse. Thank you for making any meal that I fancied too. I don't think we will ever forget the endless tuna and pickled onion sandwiches I craved, and that you kindly served to me. You would always go that step further though and present my odd cravings to me like a fine-dining dish. It was those touches that made me smile throughout my treatment. If I fancied Welsh cakes or pancakes you would make them in a heartbeat. Thank you for being just the best, Mum.

## Dad

Thanks, Dad, for being the first one up in the morning and being ready on hand for anything that needed doing that day. You did our ironing, walked the dog and did odd jobs around the house. You brought humour when it was needed and would sit with me and watch boring TV programmes to pass the day. Where there was a need, you filled it. Muffin loved you and even the postman and couriers soon became your pals! Again, you are the best, Dad.

You both spent the whole five months making sure I didn't
need or want for anything and I know your care made a difference to how I coped with the treatment. Your love for me,
Darren and the kids meant so much to us and you really were
both such a blessing . . . We all love you both very much.
Thank you.

**Leighton, Karen, Ffion and Max – my brother,
sister-in-law and family**

A big thank you for all your prayers and support. I know we
don't live close to each other and so I don't see you all as much
as I would like. However, I know you are always just a message
or phone call away, and you were thinking and praying for me
constantly throughout my journey. Thank you for being such
a lovely 'Bruv' to me, Leighton. I have so many great memories from our childhood – from you not allowing me in your
bedroom *ever*, and me owning your nickname for me of 'bossy
flossy'. I just want to say I love and appreciate you all and let's
visit each other more, please!

**Pam and Dave – my in-laws**

Through my treatment I wasn't able to visit you both, and
I know that you were concerned and wanted to help in so
many ways (as you always do) and that, Pam, it was difficult
for you. Thank you both for your constant love to me as a
daughter-in-law. I know, Pam, that this has been a tough season for you too, in caring for Dave, but everyone knows what

a selfless, loving person you are – an example to us all. We are all so grateful to you both for all you've done (and do!) for us. I just wanted to say how much you mean to us too. We love you lots.


**Bryan, Nicola, Emily and Nia – my in-laws**

Again we don't always see you as much as we would like due to distance but we all know we are there for each other when needed. Thank you all for your love, support and care throughout last year – I really did appreciate your prayers. Bryan – thank you for giving us endless entertainment, you are a true sport! Love you all.


**Aunties – for all my lovely aunties**

Thank you for your prayers, cards, gifts and phone calls. Your support and love meant so much to me. The way you kept checking up on me! I am grateful for my wider family too. Love you all.


**My cousins – too many to name but you know who you are!**

We are all so spread out now that it's hard to see each other but when something affects one of us, I love how we are instantly all there for each other – even if we do have to communicate by text and messages! Thank you for the constant care and prayers. You stood with me through this and showed how much you love and care for me. I appreciated you all so much. Love you all.

## My church family

I just wanted to say thank you for being such a loving and supporting church, and for the way you have given me space to recover – Darren and I have both appreciated it so much. You are all such a caring, wonderful church – thank you all so much.

## The Aspire team

I have always said I have the best team around me, and it's true! The way you gathered around me to lift me up in prayer and stood by me through my health battle, you girls are not only the best team but such valued friends. For your love, faith, prayers and laughs! Thank you so, so much.

## My friends – far and wide

I know I don't have space to thank you all personally so please know that, if you contacted me, visited me, sent me any cards, prayed for me, sent me messages or gifts, these words of thanks are to each and every one of you. Some friends that I perhaps worked with or lost contact with down the years suddenly made contact with me again during this time and I want you to know how much that meant to me. Those friends and leaders from Elim, those friends from any part of my life growing up – each one of you, I value you so much. To Gail, Winnie and Muthoni – friends who go way back and are always there for each other – thank you for meeting on Zoom to pray for me throughout my treatment. Your love spoke volumes to me. You will always remain 'chikadees'. Love to you all.

**NHS**

I am in awe. Thank you.

# Notes

1   Tania M. Harris, *God Conversations: Stories of How God Speaks and What Happens When We Listen* (Milton Keynes: Authentic Media, 2017).

2   Julia Lawton, *The End of the Beginning* (Imagine Publishing House, 2021).

3   S. Schapp, N. Gardiner and A. Baxter, 'Your Name' (Live). (Bradford: LIFE Worship, 2020).

4   Ian Yates and Tim Williams, 'I Have a Saviour', © 2021 Elim Sound Publishing (Admin Song Solutions) CCLI# 7170483, Album: *God is Still Moving.*

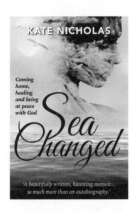

## Sea Changed

*Coming home, healing and being at peace with God*

*Kate Nicholas*

Growing up with a strong sense of spirituality, Kate searched long and hard throughout the world to make sense of that spiritual longing. After catching glimpses of the divine in many cultures along the way, Kate finally found God and her life was transformed for ever.

Kate has had some personal battles to face, including the loss of both her parents, the loss of a baby, and debilitating ME. She has battled breast cancer, from which she has been miraculously healed.

*Sea Changed* encourages readers to recognise the unseen hand that shifts our perspective, alters our trajectory and lifts us up even in our darkest moments.

978-1-78078-162-4

**Hope Wins**

*How a vision of our eternal future
impacts our lives today*

*Goff Hope*

Hope is fundamental for human wellbeing but it is in short supply
in our world. We can quickly be robbed of hope by illness, personal
tragedy or by the sheer oppressive nature of news headlines.

Drawing on his own personal experiences, including the tragedy of
losing his daughter and his own battle with cancer, Goff shares how
holding on to the Christian hope of an eternal future transformed the
darkest moments of his life.

Interweaving personal testimony of the goodness of God with biblical
teaching on heaven, Goff encourages us to see that when tough times
come, and we are tempted to doubt or ask the big questions, such as
Why, Lord?, we can have hope if we keep our eyes on Jesus and have a
heavenly perspective on life.

978-1-78893-276-9

**Be – Godly Wisdom to Live By**

*365 devotions for women*

*Fiona Castle and friends*

Jesus gave us the greatest love of all. We are called not just to keep it to ourselves, but to overflow with that love to others. But how can we really do that in the busyness of our lives?

In these daily devotions, women from many walks of life share insights on scripture and practical life lessons to gently encourage you to live for Jesus, and to be more like him in your thoughts, character, and actions.

Discover godly wisdom that will help you navigate the world as a Christian woman and live out God's unique purpose for your life.

978-1-78893-239-4

**Safe All Along**

*Trading our fears and anxieties for
God's unshakable peace*

*Katie Davis Majors*

As a missionary, wife, and mum of fifteen, Katie Davis Majors knows
how hard it can be to receive God's peace instead of giving in to fear
and worry. Family emergencies, unexpected life-shifting events, and
the busy rhythms of family life have at times left her reeling.

In *Safe All Along*, Katie offers reflections and stories from around the
world and from her own kitchen table about her personal journey
toward living from a place of surrendered trust. Every chapter leads us
deep into Scripture as we learn what it looks like to break free from
anxiety and take hold of peace.

Our God has promised us a peace that transcends all understanding.
And we can accept his promise, trusting that in him we are safe all
along.

978-1-78893-316-2

**Salt Water and Honey**

*Lost dreams, good grief,
and a better story*

*Lizzie Lowrie*

Reeling from the disappointment of a failed business venture, Lizzie Lowrie's life takes a nightmarish turn as she suffers miscarriage after miscarriage.

Written from the messy middle of life, where there are no neat or cliched answers, Lizzie honestly shares her pain and the fight to find God in her suffering.

Providing a safe space to remind people that they're not alone, it's okay to grieve and their story matters, this is for anyone who has lost their dream and is struggling to understand their purpose when life looks nothing like they hoped it would.

978-1-78893-095-6

## Postcards from the Land of Grief

*Comfort for the journey through loss towards hope*

*Richard Littledale*

Losing a loved one can be a lonely, isolating and disorientating experience. Written as postcards from this land of grief, Richard Littledale honestly shares his personal experience in an accessible way that helps fellow travellers to identify their feelings and find hope in the foreign country of bereavement.

Thought-provoking, honest, gentle and ultimately hope-filled, this is a helpful companion for anyone dealing with loss.

978-1-78893-071-0

**Authentic**

We trust you enjoyed reading this book from Authentic. If you want to be informed of any new titles from this author and other releases you can sign up to the Authentic newsletter by scanning below:

Online:
authenticmedia.co.uk

Follow us: